COACH OF A
DIFFERENT COLOR

SERIES ON OHIO HISTORY AND CULTURE

Series on Ohio History and Culture
    Kevin Kern, Editor

Kathleen Endres, *Akron's "Better Half": Women's Clubs and the
    Humanization of a City, 1825–1925*

Russ Musarra and Chuck Ayers, *Walks Around Akron: Rediscovering a
    City in Transition*

Heinz Poll, edited by Barbara Schubert, *A Time to Dance: The Life of
    Heinz Poll*

Mark D. Bowles, *Chains of Opportunity: The University of Akron and
    the Emergence of the Polymer Age, 1909–2007*

Russ Vernon, *West Point Market Cookbook*

Stan Purdum, *Pedaling to Lunch: Bike Rides and Bites in Northeastern Ohio*

Joyce Dyer, *Goosetown: Reconstructing an Akron Neighborhood*

Robert J. Roman, *Ohio State Football: The Forgotten Dawn*

Timothy H. H. Thoresen, *River, Reaper, Rail: Agriculture and Identity in
    Ohio's Mad River Valley, 1795–1885*

Brian G. Redmond, Bret J. Ruby, and Jarrod Burks, eds., *Encountering
    Hopewell in the Twenty-first Century, Ohio and Beyond. Volume 1:
    Monuments and Ceremony*

Brian G. Redmond, Bret J. Ruby, and Jarrod Burks, eds., *Encountering
    Hopewell in the Twenty-first Century, Ohio and Beyond. Volume 2:
    Settlements, Foodways, and Interaction*

Jen Hirt, *Hear Me Ohio*

Ray Greene, *Coach of a Different Color*

Titles published since 2006.
For a complete listing of titles published in the series,
    go to www.uakron.edu/uapress.

COACH OF A DIFFERENT COLOR

ONE MAN'S STORY OF BREAKING BARRIERS IN FOOTBALL

Ray Greene

The University of Akron Press
Akron, Ohio

ISBN: 978-1-629221-22-9 (paper)
ISBN: 978-1-629221-85-4 (ePDF)
ISBN: 978-1-629221-86-1 (ePub)

A catalog record for this title is available from the Library of Congress.

∞The paper used in this publication meets the minimum requirements of ANSI/NISO
z39.48–1992 (Permanence of Paper).

Cover: Kenmore Football Team, courtesy of the author. Cover design by Amy Freels.

Coach of a Different Color was designed and typeset in Utopia by Amy Freels and printed on
sixty-pound white and bound by Bookmasters of Ashland, Ohio.

Contents

Introduction
The Future Is Now

Rosa Parks sat on a front seat of a bus in Montgomery, Alabama.

Autherine Lucy entered the University of Alabama after Governor George Wallace stood in the doorway attempting to block her entrance.

The Little Rock Nine, over Governor Oral Faubus' strenuous objections, integrated Little Rock Central High School.

President John F. Kennedy was assassinated on November 22, 1963.

On March 7, 1965, Dr. Martin Luther King Jr. led a march for voting rights from Selma, Alabama, to Montgomery, Alabama, that would lead them over the Edmund Pettus Bridge. The bridge was named after Edmund Pettus who, at one time, was the leader of the KKK. That event became known as "Bloody Sunday."

Martin Luther King Jr. was murdered on April 4, 1968.

Robert F. Kennedy was murdered on June 5, 1968.

Three young men—James Chaney, Andrew Goodman, and Michael Schwerner—were murdered in Philadelphia, Mississippi, on June 21, 1964, while fighting for voting rights.

These and countless others risked and gave their lives to achieve equality for black Americans. They were true patriots who will be remembered in history for their bravery and their fight for equal justice and voting rights.

*

Being a football coach, no matter the struggles or accomplishments, pales in the shadows of those who paid the ultimate price to make our country live up to its promise of freedom and justice for all.

My story is not one of sacrifice. Although I did receive death threats and worried about my family's safety, there was no open hostility toward them or me on a regular basis. My story had its genesis in the courage of young black men at universities across the nation. Buoyed by the protests in America and abroad, they were the ones who had the real courage to stand up and make reasonable demands of their coaches, colleges, and universities. They took the risks and stood tall against established policies. Many lost scholarships and were disdained by the press, but they would not be deterred.

Will future generations, as they study history lessons about the 1960s, gain a clear understanding of the tenor of the times and the turmoil that led to death and division in America? Will they take up the banner and make the ultimate sacrifice as so many did before them? Those questions remain unanswered; however, to truly understand the situation, it is important to study the political, economic, religious, intellectual, and aesthetic viewpoints in our society during those times.

"It was the best of times, it was the worst of times." The quote from Charles Dickens' *A Tale of Two Cities* succinctly describes the period in America between 1963 and 1969. Americans black, white, young, and old were exercising the freedom to protest and demand a change of direction for the country. It was a time of self-expression and individuality. I was fortunate to be part of that change. But the tragic events mentioned earlier also show that it was the worst of times. Future generations, hopefully, will find it unbelievable that those things could have happened in this country.

These and other events in American history are mostly footnotes in the curriculum of the nation's schools. Students know more about ISIS than they know about America's own history of terrorism. Textbooks give only a cursory view of heinous acts committed against Native Americans and the atrocities committed during and after slavery.

Coaching and teaching young people provides an opportunity to teach more than what is included in textbooks or how to play a game. I had many in-depth discussions with our athletes about current issues, hoping to pique their interest so they would be motivated to learn more on their own. Honest and open discussions could prepare them for leadership roles that could change the race divide in America. However, recent events some half-century later show that there is still much work to be done.

When Barack Obama was elected president, many whites thought we had reached a point in our society where, finally, we had overcome the divisiveness. Now it is clear that Obama's election did not solve the problem. Instead it was the catalyst that allowed the racial divide to rise to the surface. During his two terms, "take back our country" became a popular dog whistle to those who feared progress.

Some politicians define the phrase in terms of illegal immigration and border security. Latinos are targeted as scapegoats for all of America's ills, similar to the way Hitler targeted Jews. Now, Muslims are also targeted. Guns are flying off the shelves and paramilitary organizations are arming themselves with high-powered weapons.

In 2015, overt racism surfaced in Charleston, South Carolina. Using his acceptance to attend Bible study at the historically black Emanuel African Methodist Episcopal Church, Dylann Roof, a twenty-one-year-old white man, walked into Bible study one evening, opened fire, and killed nine members of the church, including a state senator. Police later found Confederate flags decorating his home. Roof also confessed that his goal was to start a race war.

Roof's deliberate actions, as horrible as they were, produced an unexpected consequence: Americans were appalled, angry, and ashamed at the same time. In the aftermath of the attack, Governor Nikki Haley went before her legislature and made an impassioned plea to remove the Confederate flags from all South Carolina state buildings. Initially, there was little opposition. Her brave stand about what flying the flag implied to blacks encouraged many cities across the South to remove the flags.

The backlash came later. Many objected, saying the flag paid homage to their ancestors who died for the Confederacy in the War Between the States. However, to many the Confederate flag had become the dominant symbol used in the 1960s to protest sweeping civil rights decisions.

The murders in Charleston were preceded by several incidents between young black men and the police. In 2012, a civilian acting as an enforcer of the law had a confrontation with an unarmed black teenager that led to the young man's murder. Trayvon Martin, just seventeen, was killed on the way home from a convenience store carrying a bag of Skittles and a soft drink. When George Zimmerman saw him and called the police, they advised him not to act on his own, but he did not listen. Today, Trayvon Martin and others are dead as racial tensions rise again.

*

Finding a complete history that details black athletes protesting their treatment at major universities is difficult. Perhaps it is because the athletic departments were embarrassed, or some did not think it important enough to be mentioned with other more publicized historical events.

However, black athletes did speak out about being treated differently from white athletes and demanded that universities hire more coaches who looked like them. Those demands paid off. To the best of my knowledge, in the spring of 1969, I was one of the first men of color to be hired at a major university as a full-time assistant football coach. I have those athletes to thank for that.

My presence on coaching staffs gave me a chance to provide my white associates at least some sense of what it feels like to be black in America. Still, it is difficult to convey all the subtle things that affected me as a black man. Even if I could describe them, many whites would dismiss them as paranoia.

They would not be wrong, but the paranoia is still justified. I worry that I will be stopped again by police, for no good reason, and maybe end up dead. I worry that an officer might mistake me for someone else they were looking for. This happened to a newly elected black councilman in Huntsville, Alabama in 2017. Luckily, he was not harmed. But if the officer had not been properly trained, he could have felt threatened, and a tragedy could have occurred.

I resented the need to feel obligated to counsel my ten-year-old son on how to react when, not if, he was stopped by the police. That was thirty-five years ago. Today, he is passing that advice on to his sons.

Paranoia among black men is not new. However, technology has enabled the world to view graphic proof of the mistreatment perpetuated on black men. Looking at the number of these recent incidents reveals just how many similar incidents in the past have been covered up.

There are documented accounts of the vicious treatment of black men from the era of slavery and Jim Crow to today. Black and white children often don't learn about it because it is excluded from textbooks. This is and has been a missed opportunity for both white and black children to understand the world around them.

Imagine a young black boy in second grade listening to his teacher and following along the stories in his book *Little Black Sambo* about a little, "nappy-headed" black boy dressed in a suit doing stupid things. I was that little boy; and even at age seven, I was ashamed. I did not know any little black boys who looked like that, but I could tell that picture about black people was embedded in the minds of white children in my class. Although that ridiculous little book originally depicted the life of an Indian boy, in America, it became the life of a black "pickaninny" that stereotyped black people.

I grew up watching Tarzan put the fear of God into the natives in the jungle. I also saw Mantan Moreland, "Stepin Fetchit," and a host of other colored people in the movies displaying stupidity and laziness. *Amos 'n' Andy*, one of my favorite TV programs, was a funny sitcom that my family and I watched each week. The main characters in the sitcom were Kingfish, who never had a job and was always trying some "get rich" scheme; Algonquin J. Calhoun, a lawyer who played a dumb attorney; Lightning, a custodian who was lazy and slow; and Andy, a cab driver who was the only sane person on the show. Although the show subtly ingrained the worst traits about blacks into the psyche of blacks and whites, the reality did not come clear to me until I was in tenth grade. I overheard a conversation between two black men who were talking about lawyers. One of them said, "I would never trust a black lawyer." I had an epiphany! They watched *Amos 'n' Andy*.

Most of the colored people I saw on television were poor, servants, criminals, and every other negative, inferior stereotype the entertainment industry could exploit. Many colored people, then, straightened their hair and some used Nadinola bleaching cream to lighten dark skin to emulate the white concept of beauty.

Thankfully, those notions have almost disappeared. The civil rights movement produced a generation of young black people like Rap Brown, Stokeley Carmichael, and Angela Davis, to name a few, who declared that "black is beautiful." Then, singer James Brown made it an anthem when he recorded "I'm Black and I'm Proud." Black became beautiful.

Unfortunately, many internalized the feelings ingrained from years of being seen as "less than." Their self-hatred led them to fight back by using and selling drugs, forming gangs, and creating a Third World culture outside of the mainstream.

That culture has lingered and is still used by politicians and the media to illustrate the "dark" side of black people. This distorted stereotype has given police officers excuses to brutalize or kill young black men and women, who are automatically seen as "threatening." A classic example of this is the Rodney King case of 1991. The Los Angeles police defense stated that the only choice was to beat him with night sticks because he would not stop moving around and because he was so big.

There have been numerous unarmed minorities killed by police officers who possess the power of life and death in carrying out their jobs. The system has allowed them to use the phrase, "I feared for my life" to absolve them of any criminal guilt even in cases where there is visual evidence of their misdeeds.

Regardless of the station he holds in life or how he dresses, a black man is seen as a threat to many whites. There is a joke among black men that, in a sense, illustrates this. "What does a white man call a black man dressed in a suit and tie?" (The answer is "Niggah!")

We tell it with humor, but it's actually an expression of mild paranoia. This doesn't necessarily mean we live forever in fear, but it demands that we are always on guard, much like gazelles wary of leopards lurking in the bushes. Unlike the gazelles, our "leopards" are in plain sight.

This is not a condemnation of white people in general. My experience with whites has always been much more positive than negative. Unfortunately, many still believe the country would be better off returning to the days of Jim Crow.

On a recent talk show on Fox News, a caller made the statement, "White lives matter." I thought it was an ignorant way to deride the Black Lives Matter movement. Of course white lives matter. However, although there may have been whites who have died while in police custody, I have seen no evidence or statistics that indicate whites have to be concerned about being choked to death on a public street for selling illegal cigarettes or shot and killed while unarmed in the middle of the street.

The caller's statement is similar to saying not all police officers are bad. Most people understand that, but if the fellow officers say or do nothing about the bad ones, are they not also complicit?

*

What does all of this have to do with me and coaching? It is the idea that many coaches at all levels back in the sixties considered black athletes too "pushy" when they demanded fair treatment, coaches who looked like them, and the same opportunities afforded their white teammates when they graduated from college.

Many athletic directors felt the same when blacks wanted to be considered for various coaching positions. In a larger sense, that type of thinking still persists throughout society if we consider the small percentage of blacks in the media, in the corporate world, and in many other institutions other than prisons. Our politicians continue to drive a wedge between blacks, whites, Latinos, and Muslims by painting a picture of gloom, doom, and fear.

The latest politician using race and ethnicity to garner votes from those who want to "take back our country" is Donald Trump. Preying on the fears of many Americans, he has all but damned Mexicans in his quest to gain support from voters who resented a black man being president. Now he has suggested keeping a database on refugees and a watch list on Muslims. He even proposed banning Muslims from entering the country. During Trump's tenure, the terms *racist* and *racism* have openly come to the surface and been thrown around indiscriminately.

Actually, I do not believe most people understand the difference between racism and prejudice. We all have our prejudices and we can choose to dislike an individual's race, religion, color, or ethnicity for whatever reason we wish. However, most of us do not have the power to act in any meaningful way to affect their lives. It becomes racism when power is given to those prejudices. The argument put forth by some that blacks are racists or promote racism is a misnomer because blacks and people of color are not in a position to hire, fire, or set limits on society at large.

Where does it all end? Are we headed for the race war that Dylann Roof wanted? I hope it will not come to that because I believe that the majority of Americans are informed people who are not locked in to one source of information. I hope I am right.

Where do we go from here? All real change begins locally. People who love and care about the future of this country could organize meetings with like-minded people of all races in their hometowns. They should have real discussions about race. Perhaps this might lead to a national initiative to begin steps toward using the power of the majority to vote and elect candidates who will do what is right rather than what is expedient.

*

This book is not a book about football, although football is prominently discussed to put in perspective my role in giving a voice, from the inside, to the athletes who were responsible for the career I wanted. As the lone black coach on all but one of the staffs I worked with in high school, Division I, and professional football, I not only had to prove my ability to coach, but I also had the unique opportunity to address many areas with fellow staff members that enabled them to gain a broader perspective and understanding of racial issues.

I have never thought of myself as just a football coach. I could not speak for all black people. However, in those nonthreatening circumstances, I know some positive outcomes occurred. Sports can't be separated from the society and the social structure that shapes our attitudes and beliefs. The multicultural environment I grew up in combined with my educational experiences became valuable assets in pursuing my goal to become a collegiate head football coach. I found those experiences helped me to dispel some stereotypes and perhaps change some attitudes in the process. No one can get inside someone else's skin, especially if the skin is of a different color. My presence on various coaching staffs enabled me to provide my associates a realistic sense of what it feels like to be black or a minority in America.

*

At the end of the 2014 collegiate football season, three of the four teams selected to participate in the inaugural BCS Championship started black athletes at quarterback. The fourth was from Hawai'i—not black, but also not white.

The Ohio State University, who won that year's National Championship, did not play their first or second-team quarterbacks, who are black, because both were injured. So, the Buckeyes had to start their third-teamer who, incidentally, is also black.

Around the nation, black quarterbacks have led successful programs at Auburn, UCLA, Mississippi State, and Alabama, to name a few. During the three or four years prior to 2014, the most productive and successful programs in the major conferences were led by black athletes playing quarterback. These days most fans and coaches don't give much thought to the color of the quarterback as long as he gets the job done.

In 1969, this was not the case. That year, Wayne Stanley, a talented black quarterback from Belle Glade, Florida, had an outstanding career at Belle Glade High School. He was clean-cut, intelligent, and qualified for admission to most of the nation's colleges. He received letters of interest from many Division I institutions and was offered athletic scholarships to many outstanding programs. He could have his pick of universities. However, there was one problem: most of the universities were projecting him to be a wide receiver or defensive back. He had all of the tools needed to play quarterback—he ran the forty-yard dash in 4.5 seconds, had a strong arm, and he played in one of the most competitive high school leagues in Florida.

I went to Belle Glade to recruit Wayne and found he was personable, well-spoken, from a good family, and was well respected in his community. His coaches said he was one of their hardest workers and a great competitor. When I viewed four or five of Stanley's game film, each one showed that he was a "thirty-footer." That expression, now obsolete, was used by coaches to mean an athlete is impressive enough in the first thirty feet of film to be signed.

I spoke with Wayne's coach, the guidance office, his minister, and the registrar's office to determine whether his off-the-field actions mirrored his athletic prowess. They did. When I met with Wayne, I offered him a scholarship and told him I would love to have him come to Iowa State to play quarterback in the Big Eight Conference.

A bit skeptical, he asked whether he would really get an opportunity to play quarterback, or would he be switched to another position. My response was, "I give you my word and promise you that you will get a fair opportunity to play quarterback at Iowa State." Evidently, he believed me, and I signed him.

Wayne had an outstanding career as a quarterback and graduated with a degree in business. At about the same time, his head coach at Iowa State, Earle Bruce, accepted the head coaching position at The Ohio State University. One of the first staff members Earle hired was twenty-one-year-old Wayne Stanley. Wayne went on to coach for nine years at Ohio State before going into private business.

After I signed Wayne, I told Coach John Majors, the head coach, in no uncertain terms that Wayne was a quarterback. After he looked at him on film, there was no denying Wayne was the best quarterback in the recruiting class.

Freshmen then could not play on the varsity, so Wayne had to split time with two other freshman quarterbacks. In the five freshmen games we played, he was clearly the best athlete in each stadium. When the freshmen practiced against the varsity, he was the best athlete on the field. Still, a few of our coaches always had something negative to say about the little things he could not do as a quarterback. They thought he would be a great cornerback or wide receiver.

I never let them off the hook. I told them I would not be able to recruit athletes from Florida if he did not get every opportunity to compete for the position. I was not going to let them, or anyone, make me break my promise to Wayne.

Whether or not there would be a controversy about Wayne became moot. In the spring of 1973, Coach Majors accepted the head coaching position at the University of Pittsburgh. Earle Bruce became the head coach at Iowa State. Earle played the best quarterback on campus—Wayne Stanley.

Today, the idea of not thinking of black athletes as quarterbacks seems almost unreal. But then, in the minds of many coaches, the idea of a black youngster leading their team was unthinkable. At the time, there were fewer black coaches in major college football than there were black quarterbacks.

In 1968, to the best of my recollection, there was only one black coach in the Big Ten—Frank Gilliam at the University of Iowa. Frank was an outstanding player at Iowa who was hired as an assistant coach after a career in Canadian football. His hiring took place before black athletes at major universities began the revolution in the 1960s that provided the impetus for black coaches' "intrusion" into major college football. Frank's hiring went under the radar primarily because of the respect his coaches had for him as a man.

Many years earlier in 1923, Jack Trice became the first black athlete to play football for Iowa State. He was killed while playing against Minnesota. During that time, few teams had black athletes and most teams refused to play opponents who had a black person on their roster. From written eyewitness accounts, it appeared that Trice, after making a play, was deliberately kicked and stepped on, which lead to his death the next day. In 1997, Iowa State named the football stadium after Trice because of a student and faculty petition. Jack Trice Stadium in Ames, Iowa, is currently the only major stadium in America named after a black man.

From its beginning, football was a white man's sport. When it became integrated, black athletes were cautioned to be seen and not heard. Coaches were dictators and what they said was law, until black athletes at San Jose State in the 1960s, under the leadership of Dr. Harry Edwards, decided to push the limits and state their grievances.

Between 1963 and 1969, America was going through turmoil on several fronts: the Vietnam War protests, the assassinations of Dr. Martin Luther King Jr. and the Kennedy brothers, desegregation of schools in the South, and the Voting Rights Act. The civil rights movement was at its zenith. Students on many campuses across America were protesting and more collegiate football rosters included substantial numbers of black athletes who played important roles in their team's success. Dr. Edward's effective protests at San Jose lit the fire that gave them the courage to publicly voice their dissatisfaction about the way they were treated by coaches and trainers. They started asserting their racial pride by growing afros and beards, and demanded the hiring of coaches who looked like them.

This did not sit well with many coaches, administrators, fans, and supporters of major programs. Several coaches displayed little tolerance and retaliated when their athletes became involved in protests. Some even made it a rule that protesting was not allowed. Football games had long made segregation and desegregation visible, and black athletes who wanted to play football learned early to avoid talking about politics. That changed in the 1960s and 1970s when black athletes identified with the broader struggle and expressed themselves in public.

In 1969, Willie Black, a black doctoral student at the University of Wyoming, invited black athletes to participate in a campus-wide protest. Knowing that there was a policy against demonstrations, some of the football players decided to talk with the coach about it. All fourteen players were dismissed instantly.

A press release from the university stated that the students would "not play in today's game or any during the balance of the season," and that "The dismissals result from a violation of a football coaching rule Friday morning."

Newspapers dubbed the dismissed players the "Black 14." When the lawsuit went to federal court, Eaton testified that he told his players that if they weren't satisfied with their program, they should probably consider going to other colleges.

The decision by Wyoming did not deter athletes protesting; it solidified their resolve. The action of young black athletes who risked losing scholarships and perhaps lucrative professional careers persuaded those in power that hiring black coaches was absolutely necessary.

Earlier I used the word *intrusion* because many head football coaches felt pressured and hired black assistants with more than a little reluctance. One consistent trait among football coaches—and coaches in general—is that they want to win. Later, in the early 1970s, after observing the success of black quarterbacks like Sandy Stephens, Jimmy Raye, Warren Moon, and Tony Dungy and the impact they had on the game, coaches began looking at black quarterbacks differently.

Football ranks low in importance by comparison, but the integration of major collegiate football coaching staffs was a major event in its own right. This book chronicles one black coach's path into the world of major college football and beyond.

Often, I thought about writing about my experience as a football coach; however, the inspiration to get started was lacking until I met Peter Bilodeau. When Peter, a former newspaperman, a devout Tennessee Vol football fan, and a freelance writer, learned how I came to work with John Majors at Iowa State, he told me the story would make a great book. I took his advice and began writing. Thank you Peter for your assistance and coaching throughout the process.

Many people contributed to whatever success I have had. However, following are those whose contributions I treasure more than they know. Pat, my wife of fifty-four years—she jogged my memory to help me fill in the blanks. John Majors hired me and provided me the opportunity to learn how to be a college coach. Thanks to the staffs with whom I worked who aided in my development as a coach and the hard-working, great people at Iowa State who befriended my family and always made us feel welcome. To the black athletes who demonstrated leadership and courage, thank you for changing the coaching profession, and finally, to the thousands of young athletes who I watched grow into productive citizens and leaders—thanks for the memories.

Special thanks to John Majors, Dwight Wright, Ray Sherman, and Jimmy Johnson who took time out of their busy schedules to write nice thoughts about me.

Chapter 1

Childhood
Much Diversity, a Few Diversions

I am not sure what some might envision as a typical black kid, and I do not know what category I fit into. Urban? Yes. Troubled? No. In trouble? Nothing major.

As a child, I obviously knew I was black (Negro or colored back then), but I never thought much about it or felt different because of it. (I use the term *Negro* or *colored* because during those times, we were not yet "black" or "African American." Those designations would come later.) I did know that black skin color was not respected and that to be light-skinned was thought to be more desirable. "Good" hair meant having straight hair like white people. Millions of dollars were spent by colored people on straightening combs and other hair products to make their "kinky" hair straight. The beneficiaries of this cash windfall, unfortunately, happened to be white corporations.

When I went to the movies, which was often, I rarely saw any black faces on the screen. The ones who were on the screen were servants or always acted stupid, scared, or ignorant. They did not act like the people in our neighborhood or other colored people I knew. However, I still felt embarrassed at how they portrayed black people. I loved to watch the Tarzan movies, starring Johnny Weissmuller. But as I watched hundreds of natives run with fear when they heard Tarzan's yell, I thought to myself that if he tried that on Miami Street, where I grew up in Akron, Ohio, he would get his ass kicked.

Thinking back, I realize now that I had really good teachers (all white) who made every effort to provide me the best education possible. They were supportive and all of them were nice, except Mrs. Brownstein, my third-grade teacher. We thought she was one mean and strict woman. However, in retrospect, it was just that she had a gruff personality and, in spite of it, I learned a lot in her class.

When I started school, there were no middle schools. Elementary school went from kindergarten to eighth grade. Then, it was on to high school. Families were not as mobile as they are now and neighborhoods were stable. We knew our neighbors and they knew us. Therefore, most of my classmates and I went from kindergarten through high school together. Our teachers knew our weaknesses and strengths and tailored their instruction to our learning styles. Because of that, we received a quality education.

My parents were not actively involved in our education except for demanding that we go to school; they never visited my schools. However, I vividly remember in first grade my mother giving me a note to take to my teacher. I couldn't read yet, so I didn't know what it said. She did the same when I started second grade.

By that time, I had learned to read—not well, but enough to decipher the note. In effect, it read "You have my permission to spank Ray or do whatever you feel is necessary if he acts up. Also, please contact me if he does and I will take care of him when he gets home." My own mother had thrown me under the bus! But I was not one to cause any problems for teachers.

My first school was Allen Elementary in South Akron. I attended Allen from 1943 to 1952. Allen was a neighborhood school. Most of the same teachers were there throughout my years at the school and they knew all the students.

We walked to school each morning. On the way, we passed by the wine store, where the local "winos" waited for it to open. We always messed with them and they would pretend to chase us. During the winter, we bombed them with snowballs—all in good fun. Still, it was a sorry sight to see grown men asking us for money to buy a sixty-cent pint of Muscatel or Mad

Dog 20/20. When we returned home from school, they were still there begging for money to buy more wine. I could not really process the situation, but it seemed really strange that these men did not have to go to work at the rubber factory every day like the other men in the neighborhood.

Akron is divided by direction: north, south, east, west, and central. Where we lived and attended high school in South Akron was close to the population center in West Akron. There was some animosity between the boys of South Akron and those in West Akron. I never knew the reason, but when we ventured to West Akron, we went in groups.

We also traveled in groups, just in case there was some trouble, to the main gathering place for young people—the Akron Community Service Center in central Akron. We did not consider ourselves a gang and we had no weapons other than our fists. We were all aware of drugs, who used them and who sold them, but we were not involved. We called ourselves the Southern Knights. At the time, we didn't know about the Knights of the Ku Klux Klan or we probably would have chosen a different name.

The center was a multipurpose facility that offered a wide variety of programs, from music and art to health, home economics, and improving workplace relations. It was a time when rock 'n' roll, doo-wop singing groups, and Elvis Presley ruled the airwaves. Many of us tried to form music groups.

We all practiced at the center. However, there was only one group that ever actually made a record. Ruby Nash formed a group named Ruby and the Romantics. They had one big hit, "Our Day Will Come." It was number one on the Top Ten charts in 1963. They never had another hit but made a good living doing what they loved—singing. Ruby's brother and I later played college football at The University of Akron and she married another one of my teammates, Robert Garnett.

We took classes in karate and arts and crafts, swam, and played basketball. Invariably, there was always someone from West Akron who wanted to challenge us either in basketball or in a fight. When we beat them in basketball, they wanted to fight. We usually won.

We never got into fights at the center because Mr. Vernon Odom and Mr. George Miller, the directors, had a no-fight policy that everyone followed. When we entered the center, we had to remove our hats. If we wanted to play basketball, we had to carry our gym shoes into the center.

We could not play on the court with the shoes we wore into the facility. No one ever debated Mr. Miller or Mr. Odom about the rules.

Everyone had the greatest respect for those two men. Mr. Odom was not only director of the center, he also was president of the Urban League and a professor at The University of Akron. Mr. Miller was Mr. Odom's assistant and ran activities in the evenings. During the day, he was an elementary school principal. These men were the first educated black men with whom I had a personal relationship. They were excellent role models for me and I think of them often when I work with youngsters.

Our contact was mostly with Mr. Miller because he ran the summer recreation program at our neighborhood Thornton Park and coached our softball team. We had great teams when we were in the sixth through eighth grades. I get a warm feeling remembering some of the guys who played. Many of us went on to earn college scholarships in football, basketball, or track.

Mr. Miller drove a 1953 Chevy convertible. It was a beautiful turquoise blue and cream color, and it was sharp. He squeezed us in the front and back seats—and the trunk—two or three times a week to go to games. By the end of summer, we had ruined his car. One day, I asked him why he allowed us to pack his car and mess it up. His answer has guided my thinking when working with young people. He said that the car was nothing but metal and leather and that he could buy another one. He went on to tell us that he loved us and wanted us to participate in positive activities and grow up to be productive adults. In effect, he told us that he cared about us.

The pupil population at Allen Elementary School was about 60–40, white to black. There were no racial problems, though students sometimes got into normal, childhood skirmishes. I had my share of fights and was often in the principal's office. The principal, Mr. Mardis Williams, a retired Army Colonel, applied what he called the "board of education" to my backside.

Mr. Williams' "board" was actually a paddle the shop teacher made for him. It was about three feet long, with several one-inch holes. When visiting Allen after I went to high school, I got the nerve to ask Mr. Williams about the holes. He smiled and told me the holes lessened the wind resistance when he swung it. Except for a few paddlings, I had very little trouble in school.

I was a good student, especially in reading and spelling. In 1953, I won our school's spelling bee and represented our district in the regional spelling bee in Cleveland, Ohio. There, the word *phlegmatic* tripped me up in the second round and I was eliminated.

My nemesis was Rose Ann Green (no relation). She always beat me when we had spelldowns. Let me amend that. In our last competition in the eighth grade, the winner of the spelldown would be chosen to compete in the city-wide competition, and I beat her. I will never forget the word—*antidisestablishmentarianism*. Rose Ann knew the word, but in the stress of the moment, she got flustered. I saw it and nailed it. In the city-wide competition I made it to the final six. The word I missed was *freight*. I have never been more upset with myself—I knew the exceptions to the "i-e" rule! Rose Ann would never have missed it. That experience taught me that remembering rules and applying them under duress can sometimes be difficult.

*

One of the most exciting times I experienced at Allen was when Bernard "Truck" Connelly became our school's first-ever basketball coach. Coach Connelly played basketball at Kent State University, fifteen miles from Akron. As my first real coach, he taught me and the rest of the team sound fundamentals.

His teaching gave our team an advantage over our competitors when we tried out for basketball at South High School. He could actually demonstrate what he was teaching us and we were able to watch him play in the city's A League. When he scored a basket or made a good play, we enjoyed letting everyone around us know that he was our coach.

Mr. Odom, Mr. Miller, and Coach Connelly treated us like their own. They were never too busy to talk to us. They asked our opinions and we felt respected. Generally, I had a great time in elementary school. I never felt that being colored was a disadvantage—or an advantage—while I was a student in public schools.

Still, the defining of race and the idea of being "less than" was subtly embedded in us as youngsters. Unfortunately, because of the education system, the idea of being "better than" was also embedded in the minds of white youngsters.

Our basketball team at Allen did not have any white players. There were white kids we played with outside of the team but, for whatever reason, they did not go out for the team. We always played hard because Coach Connelly demanded it. However, when we competed against predominately white teams, there seemed to be an unspoken urgency to play harder and beat them. We usually did.

In thirteen years of public school and through undergraduate school, I had only two black teachers. One was Mrs. Dunnigan. She substituted at Allen School and we only saw her two or three times a semester. She also owned a convenience store and gas station.

None of the colored students in her class liked her because she acted as though she thought she was better than us. When our class acted up, which usually happens with a substitute teacher, Mrs. Dunnigan would often say, with an attitude of superiority, things like, "I got mine and it is up to you to get yours."

In retrospect, she was right, but she didn't seem to want to help us "get ours." The other black teacher was Mr. Berry, the woodshop teacher at South High. Mr. Berry was a very good instructor and a regular guy. Everyone liked and respected him. I still use the skills I learned from him and still have a cedar chest I made in his class. I also made some money selling several other pieces that I made in his class.

Everyone in our neighborhood expected us to play football for the South High School Cavaliers. They had a great team and some great players. My brothers, Chester and Avery, both played long before I did. They were twenty-four and twenty-six years older than me. They loved South and football. Therefore, playing football at South was the goal for the other boys in my family—my three nephews and me. Two of my nephews, Bobby and Billy, were twins and William was the other. All three were born to my two sisters in the same year three months apart. I was born a year and a half before them. I was their uncle, but we grew up more like brothers.

Before playing high school football, we played football for the South Akron Rangers, a youth league team. I was small but had good speed and ball skills. My only concern while playing in the youth league was whether I would ever get big enough to play in high school. I weighed only 105 pounds when I was ten years old. When I got to high school at age fourteen, I was only 138 pounds.

OUR NEIGHBORHOOD

Our South Akron neighborhood was a perfect example of the African adage, "it takes a village to raise a child." Everyone knew each other. If we were caught doing anything naughty, it was not unusual to get a spanking from any parent who saw it. Not only did our parents approve of the other parents' actions, we usually got a second dose of punishment when we got home.

The neighborhood was like a United Nations of ethnicities. There were whites, Italians, Hungarians, Germans, and a family of Cubans. My parents moved to Akron from Marshallville, Georgia. They did what many black families did—move north for better opportunities. In Akron, the opportunity was rubber. Akron was once called "The Rubber Capital of the World" because the headquarters of every major rubber company in the world (Goodyear, Goodrich, Firestone, Seiberling, Mohawk, etc.) was located there.

My dad worked at Firestone Tire & Rubber for thirty-five years. My oldest brother, Chester, initially worked at Firestone but quit to become a master presser at Portman's Dry Cleaning. Mr. Portman taught him how to press clothes and he became very skilled at it. Avery joined the Marines. After my dad retired from Firestone, he got bored just hanging around— and my mother told him he needed to get out of the house—so he picked up two other jobs. He worked in construction by day. That job eventually cost him his life, when a steel beam fell on him while he was helping build a freeway overpass.

In the evenings and on weekends, he had a trash route. He purchased an old truck that was so ragged and rusty it was embarrassing, but it ran well. I worked with him after school and on Saturdays. We picked up all sort of things—refrigerators, furniture, etc. I made pretty good money working eight or ten hours a week.

The northern factories offered great promise for southern blacks. Jobs were plentiful and easy to get. In fact, there's an old joke that goes, "When a colored person dies in the South, instead of going to heaven, he wanted to go to Detroit."

Many of my relatives migrated to Detroit and worked in the automobile factories. I never asked my parents why they chose to move to Akron. I was the youngest of five children and the only one born in the north. In addition to my two brothers, I had two sisters, Gladys and Eunice. Gladys was the oldest child and Eunice was two years younger. My dad was born in 1898 and my mother was born in 1900. Both were born in Marshallville, Georgia, and neither went beyond the third grade in school.

They could not provide much assistance with my schooling. However, their lack of formal education was not a testament to their innate intelligence—their insight into complicated matters often surprised me even while I was in college.

My mother was legally blind, but she used talking books to educate herself. I often listened with her to lessons on history, religion, and other subjects. She would tell me stories about working in the cotton fields of Georgia and harvesting sweet potatoes. I never understood how difficult that job was until I moved south and actually picked a piece of cotton out of a bulb. I can't imagine how difficult it must have been picking cotton ten to twelve hours a day. My mother's primary goal for me was to finish high school because none of my brothers or sisters had done so.

My parents never visited my elementary or high school except when I graduated. Though they did not feel comfortable visiting my schools, they had great respect for teachers and education.

Gladys, my older sister, became an evangelical minister and Eunice, perhaps the smartest in the family, had her own little hustle. She played host to card games. Every Friday and Saturday evening, she would have ten to fifteen regulars come to her house to gamble.

She would sell beer and liquor and take a five percent cut from each pot. I was amazed that she could figure out the five percent in her head so quickly. I worked for her on many Saturdays while in grade school and high school. I would serve customers beer or a shot of cheap liquor and bring them her famous fish sandwiches. She made a lot of money, and for a youngster, I made a lot of money. Of course, this was all illegal, but she never got any flak from the police. I figured she must have had some arrangement because they certainly knew what was going on.

When I started college, I stopped working for her because I was afraid of the bad publicity—and perhaps the end of my athletic career—if the police ever raided her games. Gladys' children were Bobby and Billy. William was Eunice's son. Eunice remarried and had eight more children. Six are college graduates and three have PhDs. Gladys' two boys chose not to continue their education after finishing high school. Bobby was an outstanding basketball player and was a starter for The University of Akron. His brother Billy was in and out of trouble but settled down and retired as a bus driver in Cleveland.

I was never a discipline problem and I would like to think that was because I was a good kid. However, it may have been because I was afraid of the punishment I would receive if I acted out. My mother, the enforcer, believed wholeheartedly in the "spare the rod, spoil the child" philosophy.

Her "rod" was three pieces of grape vine that I had to retrieve from our back yard. She would braid them into a whip-like device designed to leave its marks on a naked behind. It did not seem right that I had to supply the weapon for my own demise. Every stroke left a serious impression.

I referred to her as the "syllable whupper" because she would talk to me as she delivered the lashes. With each lash, she delivered a soliloquy without contractions: "Did-I-not-tell-you-to-straight-ten-up-your-bed-room-be-for-you-went-out-side?" Today, the "whuppings" she administered would be considered child abuse. Adrian Peterson, the great running back for the Minnesota Vikings, was suspended in 2014 for administering a similar punishment to his child, although I am sure he was not as brutal as my mother was. I believe my mother's method of discipline made me a better man.

Growing up, I do not recall ever seeing a black patrol officer; but, there were two black detectives, Archie Bullock and Jim Craig, who spent a lot of time in our neighborhood. I never knew their last names. They knew everyone and everyone knew them. I had several run-ins with the two of them, but the incidents were minor. For example, before soft drink delivery trucks were designed with covers on the sides to secure them, the drinks were delivered in open-sided trucks. Often while the delivery man was unloading soft drinks on one side, my nephews and I would be unloading drinks on the other side. It was good while it lasted.

Most of the people in our neighborhood played the numbers, even though it was illegal. Playing the numbers meant writing down three numbers on a slip of paper, much like today's Pick 3 in the lottery and placing a bet of any amount on them. Everyone hoped his number would hit because the payout was 8–1—bet $1, get $8, bet $10, get $80 etc.

There were few big winners. I learned later that it was run by the Mafia. The bookie in our neighborhood was a one-legged man called Rip. Rip could move nearly as fast on one leg and a crutch as most people could with two legs; however, he could not outrun Archie and Craig. So, he paid us to pick-up and deliver the betting slips. Archie and Craig were on to us and on several occasions would try to catch us carrying the slips. They could not charge anyone with a crime unless he was caught with the slips.

We outran them. It was the first situation in which my speed came in handy. The officers knew what we were doing and warned us that one day, they would catch us. But, they never did and never could.

There were no video games back then so, during the summer, we hung out at Thornton Park or the outdoor basketball court at Allen School. We only went home to eat. Sometimes we swam at Summit Lake or at the community center. It's a miracle we didn't get sick swimming in the lake, since the rubber factories had polluted it.

The park, such as it was, was always available; during the summer we played on the basketball court which was literally a patch of dirt with a rim on a telephone post. We had to be very careful driving for layups. We played football and baseball on our neighborhood streets. You have to be pretty tough and a bit stupid to play tackle football on concrete. Before playing in high school, one of the major games we played and looked forward to each year was on Thanksgiving. In the snow, we would play a tackle football game, without pads, against the boys from the West Side. We also did a lot of fishing; however, we did not have fancy fishing rods. We made poles out of sturdy tree branches. We could buy line, leader, and hooks for ten or fifteen cents and we dug for our own worms to use as bait. Amazingly, we actually caught fish.

Often, we went downtown to explore the two big department stores, O'Neil's and Polsky's. There were no malls then. Both stores had four floors and we explored every inch of them. Store security guards sometimes followed us around, but we were never stopped or hassled.

It is different today. In Huntsville, Alabama, where I live now, black teenagers used to go to the mall on Friday and Saturday nights to hang out. The mall manager instituted a rule that teenagers had to be accompanied by an adult if they were in the mall after six p.m. on weekends.

To my knowledge, there had never been a major problem before the rule. I did not understand the rationale unless they thought teenagers were disrupting business. I think black teenagers were targeted. However, in the process they also had to apply the rule to white youngsters. That unintended consequence led to them rescinding the rule.

Meanwhile, back in Akron, after checking out the stores, we'd sneak into a movie. In those days, the theaters would show two feature movies, a serial, and cartoons. We had two techniques: wait for the end of one movie and walk in as the crowd walked out or pay for one person's ticket and he would sneak us in through an unguarded exit door.

Occasionally, we got caught because, as the door opened, light would come in and the ushers would see us. Most of the time, though, we succeeded, because we had adjusted our technique and waited until it was dark outside. I loved the movies because they provided an escape to places I'd never seen. My favorites were scary films like *Wolfman*, *Frankenstein*, and westerns, especially with Roy Rogers and Lash LaRue. I also liked the big musicals like *Singin' in the Rain* and *Oklahoma*.

Tarzan movies were always interesting to me. In the Tarzan movies, Tarzan's yell would strike fear into hundreds of black natives. Why would they be afraid of one white guy? I know he would not have survived in my neighborhood. I guess even then, I understood the difference between fantasy and reality. Even more amazing is that I actually rooted for Tarzan. That attitude is what I came to realize as self-hatred. I identified more with Tarzan than the natives because he was white even though I had no relationship to either except the natives looked like me.

Though Archie and Craig never caught us running numbers slips, they eventually got us in a less serious matter. One cold evening, my nephews and I thought we had successfully sneaked into the Thornton Theater on Main Street. About five minutes into the movie, the theater manager came to where we were sitting and told us to come with her.

When we got to the lobby, she asked us for our ticket stubs. I lied and told her that I had bought the tickets and must have dropped them somewhere in the theater. Then, she asked the question that got us caught: "How long have you been in here?" One of my big-mouthed nephews, Bobby, spoke first and I knew immediately that we were sunk. "We've been here for more than an hour."

He should have kept quiet! She called him over to her and grabbed his ears. She said, "You are lying! Your ears are cold, and if you had been here more than an hour, they would not be." I pleaded with her not to report us, promising we'd never sneak in again. She showed no mercy. She went into her office, while another employee blocked the exit. A few minutes later, Archie and Craig walked in and gave us the "we finally got you" look.

Everyone was silent on the way home as we sat in the back seat of the unmarked police car. As the car pulled into my driveway, Craig, a huge light-skinned black man, turned on the red light. Evidently, my mother was in the living room and saw it. She walked out on the porch and saw them pulling us out of the back seat of the car. She calmly told us to "Go in the house." It was the calm before the storm. For a short time, she remained on the porch talking to the two detectives. When she entered the house, we were sitting quietly on the couch knowing what was about to happen but hoping for sympathy. I should have just gone outside to pick the vines to get it over with. After that incident, I stopped running numbers and never tried to sneak into *that* theater again.

However, I did have a traumatic experience at another theater. On Saturdays, I would head out in the morning, shoeshine box strapped across my shoulder and go downtown to make some money shining shoes. Many of the men who worked the third shift at the factories would gather at the bars to relax after a hard week's work.

Most of the time, my nephews went with me. We were only eleven or twelve years old, but usually the bar employees would not kick us out when we entered the bars to solicit shines. We got a lot of business and good tips. In about four or five hours of work, we could make fifteen or twenty dollars. That was big money to us, especially considering that the minimum wage was only seventy-five cents an hour back then.

After finishing business for the day, we would eat and then go to the community center to play basketball for a couple of hours. Then, it was off to the movies. On South Main Street there were two theaters near our neighborhood, the Thornton and the Tivoli. The Tivoli box office was right on the street, which made it hard to sneak in. However, they always showed three or four movies and cartoons, so the fifteen cents to get in was well worth it.

After playing basketball, we rushed to get to the theater in time for the start of the six p.m. movie. On this Saturday, my nephews wanted to go, but told me they had to be home before dark. So, I went by myself. I bought some popcorn, candy, and a drink and settled in to watch the movies. Sometime between when I went into the theater and when the third movie began, I fell asleep. When I woke up, I was by myself in a huge empty theater.

It was so dark I could barely see my hand in front of my face. First, fear set in and I sat there pondering what to do. After a while, my eyes became accustomed to the dark. That was even scarier because I was in a cavernous empty building by myself. I got up and walked to the front of the building and tried to open the front door. It was locked. I ran back down to the aisle, jumped on the stage, and went through the curtains to see whether there was a back entrance. I found the door, but it was also locked. I began to panic as I found my way back through the curtain and headed back to the front to try the door again. It was still locked.

It was at that moment that I realized I was hungry again, so I went to the concession stand and ate candy and stale popcorn and had a couple of soft drinks. It was about midnight, and I knew my mother would be waiting for me if I ever did get home. I knew she had talked to my nephews and I hoped she had not called the police. The last thing I wanted was another ride home with Archie and Craig.

By this time, my eyes had become accustomed to the dark and because of the red exit lights, I could see everything clearly, so I headed down to the stage. I went back to the exit door behind the curtain and saw that above the door was one of those push out windows that I could get through if I could reach it. That was a problem. I was too short to reach it. I frantically surveyed the area on the stage looking for something to stand on so I could reach the window.

Partially hidden away behind some boxes, I saw a ladder. I was in luck. I took the ladder to the door and climbed up to the window above the door. With all the strength I had, I tried to open it, but it would not budge. There was only one option left: I had to break the glass so I could climb through it. Back down the ladder I went, looking for something to break the glass. The only thing I saw were two loose weights near the end of the curtain.

I guess they used the weights on the pulleys to part the large curtain on the stage. I picked one up and went back up the ladder. At first, I gently tapped the glass, but it did not break. Then, in my frustration, I just knocked the hell out of it. The sound of glass hitting the street in the alley behind the theater sounded enormous and echoed around the theater. Someone must have heard me.

I waited a moment for the police to show up, but they didn't. The hole still wasn't big enough. Desperate, I hit the window again. This time the whole damn thing fell out with an enormous crash of glass. I dropped my shoeshine box through the hole first, and crawled through the opening, being careful not to cut myself. I jumped to the ground and started running toward home, which was about ten minutes away. About halfway there, I stopped to rest and discovered that I had small cuts on my arms and neck. I took one of my shoeshine rags and cleaned up the blood as much as possible and continued home. This would be hard to explain.

When I got home, as I expected, mama was waiting with whip in hand.

*

With fall and the beginning of school approaching I, like most kids, got some new school clothes. However, we also shopped at the Goodwill stores. I still shop there sometimes—lots of good bargains. Fall was also the beginning of football season and on Friday evenings, we would take the bus to the Rubber Bowl—a city-owned stadium—to watch high school football. We would look for discarded transfers at the local bus stops and use them. We had learned how to ride the bus all day when we wanted to without paying.

My childhood was largely trouble-free, but many of my experiences began to shape my ability to navigate the world around me and would eventually help me in my coaching career.

Chapter Two

Football, Sports Trump Music

I played football for the youth league's South Rangers for four years and could not wait to go to South High and play for the Cavaliers. In high school, in addition to football, I participated in choir, track, basketball, and a couple of school clubs. I also played the xylophone in a band.

My mother let me start taking piano lessons when I was ten, hoping that I would play for the church someday. I did play for the junior choir for a while, but that ended badly. Reverend William Carter, our minister, got upset with me because one Sunday, during the junior choir's performance, I played "Amazing Grace" and added just a little bit of a beat to it. The church clapped and tapped their feet to the music and the choir and everyone, but Reverend Carter was having a Gospel moment. I saw him give me that "what do you think you are doing" look as I got up from the piano and headed back to my seat.

As I passed the rows of church members, several told me "good job, boy." After church, Reverend Carter called out, "Greene, come up here." Out of earshot of everyone, he told me he did not want me to play a church song as if I were playing in a nightclub. "Play the music just as it is written!" he said. I left without saying anything, except "yes sir!" A few weeks later, I quit the choir not because of his admonition of me, but because they were only giving me five dollars a week, when they were paying the senior choir pianist twenty-five dollars. Admittedly, she deserved it because she played twice as well as me. Church music was not my thing, especially the way Reverend Carter wanted me to play it. My mother was incensed, but she did not make me go back to the choir.

My playing was influenced by the jazz musicians on Howard Street in downtown Akron. After my Saturday morning piano lessons downtown, I would walk the two blocks to Howard Street where several jazz clubs were located. At that time of the morning, many of the musicians were practicing for their gigs that evening.

I would sneak in and listen. I was amazed at their skill, technique, and what came out of their instruments. I often wondered who made some of these odd-looking characters practice. It was a while before I realized that they played and practiced because they loved and were passionate about the music.

Sometime later, I was looking through *Downbeat* magazine and found an article containing an interview with Miles Davis, the great jazz trumpeter. Davis mentioned there that he practiced eight to ten hours a day. That was my first understanding of the importance of passion. It drives you to overcome barriers to success. Nearly everyone has something they love doing. However, few people possess the necessary passion about what they love to become great at doing it. Although I didn't know it at the time, this would become one of the building blocks of my coaching philosophy.

Though I still loved jazz and playing piano, my passion for football and sports trumped that for music in terms of where I wanted to focus my time and effort at that time. So, after a couple of years, I quit piano lessons. I still regret it. My mother's money was not totally wasted on lessons because as an adult I took lessons again and I still play pretty well. Part of me wishes I had done more with music. I'll never know where it might have led me.

*

We had good coaches at South High School. They were all white but strangely, it never crossed my mind or seemed unusual to me. All of the other schools in the city had white coaches.

I was a big Cleveland Browns fan and I never saw any black coaches on any of the professional teams. Since most of the star players were black, that struck me as unusual, but not inappropriate. It was the same in basketball. All of the coaches and most of the players at that time, especially in professional basketball, were white. I thought the coaches were fair and the best athletes always got the most playing time. I learned later, however, that my assessment was not entirely accurate.

Gordon Larson (who played at South with my older brother, Chester) was my first high school coach. Coach Larson was a strict disciplinarian. When I was a freshman, he cut me from the team prior to the beginning of the season. South High School did not have an on-campus practice field, so we rode the bus to and from practice each day. On the third day of two-a-day practices, I overslept. When I arrived at school, the bus was leaving. Coach Larson saw me but ignored me standing there as the bus drove off. I stood there for a moment before going to the locker room to wait for the team's return from practice.

It was nearly three hours later when the bus pulled into the parking lot. Coach Larson saw me and told me to wait. When most of the team had dressed and left, he called me into his office. His comments were brief and to the point. "If you aren't responsible enough to get up on time, I can't trust you to be a responsible member of this team." I wanted to plead my case, but in those days youngsters did not argue with adults. I left the office wondering how I would explain the situation to my brothers. They never asked and I never told them why I was not playing for the Cavaliers.

I was devastated. I went to every game and had to watch from the stands. That year of sitting out changed my whole outlook on punctuality. CPT, or "colored people's time," refers to a stereotype attributed to black people that infers that black people are always late. Of course, that's not true, but at age fourteen I learned a hard lesson and I have seldom been late for anything since.

The next season, I was not in the starting lineup, but I still played a lot. After losing to Buchtel in October, we fell to 1-2 in the City Series and did not look like a playoff team. We then began winning and as underdogs won game after game. We faced Garfield in the City Championship. They were going for their third straight title. Garfield had a great team, and no one expected us to win; but, our coaches did an outstanding job of preparing us and we beat a superior opponent because of our coach's effort. Their prior planning and preparation (PPP) taught me a valuable lesson I never forgot while preparing teams during my coaching career.

Coach Larson left South to become the head coach at Marion Harding High School in southern Ohio. He eventually went on to The Ohio State University to be an assistant under Woody Hayes, the Buckeyes' legendary head coach. Later, our paths would cross again.

One of Coach Larson's assistants, Bill Hawkins, became the head coach. He was a good man, but his ability as a coach left something to be desired. We only won four games my senior year. It was disappointing, but I had to regroup because basketball season had already started and several of us on the football team had to get in basketball shape.

Our basketball team was really good. Coach Bill Satterlee was considered one of the best coaches in Ohio, and he demanded excellence. I first met him when I was in eighth grade. He came to Allen School to talk to our basketball team about what to anticipate when we tried out for basketball at South. A couple of things that he said stuck in my mind. First, in order to play on his team, we had to practice enough to know we could make a left- or right-handed lay-up every time we drove to the basket. Second, we needed to be in excellent physical condition because at South we would have to play man-to-man press defense, end-to-end, for the whole game.

I was not among the best shooters on the team, but I was not terrible. I played defense and did a good job rebounding as a two-guard. I did not start, but I played a lot and my assignment was always to guard the other team's best guard. I did what I was asked and played my role well.

Basketball provided me some valuable lessons. In basketball, a coach has less control than in football because of the nature of the game. The big difference is that in football, there is a stoppage between each play. That gives a coach the opportunity to substitute or call a play. In basketball, the point guard is like a coach on the floor and the other players have to carry out their responsibilities within the framework of the system.

Playing basketball taught me the importance of role-playing within the team. Coach Satterlee's technique of creating personnel "mismatches" became ingrained in my psyche. His teaching eventually shaped my philosophy of the passing game in football. For example, in basketball, the best situation for a player is to match him up against a lesser opponent. If that is not possible, then you try to create a two-on-one or a three-on-two situation. The same principle applies to the passing game in football.

Our team played well enough during the regular season to get a first-round bye in the district tournament, which we won. Winning the district qualified us for the regional finals. In the first round of the regionals, we played Canton McKinley.

East High School, another school from Akron, played Dayton Belmont, a team from southern Ohio. Although we were not a big team, our press and team discipline wore down McKinley and we won by six points. After our game, we showered and rushed back out to see who we would be playing the next evening. We had not seen Belmont, but we had beaten East twice during the regular season. Even though Dayton had an unimpressive-looking group of players, they played well together and won the game by two points. When we got back to our rooms, we just knew we were a better team than Dayton. We started speculating about who we would be playing in the semifinals after we beat them. That was a big mistake.

The next evening when we took the court, we were very confident. However, when the game started it was like someone put a cover over the rim. Nothing we shot went in, but everything they put up went in. Early in the second quarter, we were down seventeen points. We cut into their lead and regrouped at halftime and made a run, but we could never close the deficit to less than six points. We lost the game. The lessons I learned from that loss were valuable: never underestimate an opponent and mental preparation is equally as important as physical preparation. Even though we were a better team, we were not mentally ready to play, and so we underestimated our opponent.

The basketball season had come to an abrupt end, so I started preparing for my last season of track. At the district track meet, I qualified for the 440-yard dash and was on the 880-yard relay team.

Spring was a busy time for seniors and the prom was coming. I already had a date, but unfortunately, I did not realize the prom was the same weekend as the state track meet. Breaking that date was one of the hardest things I have ever had to do, but I couldn't miss my last chance to compete in the state track meet. After that unfortunate debacle, not only did I not win my race, I didn't even place. I was just one of the "also-rans."

I graduated from high school later that spring. My mother, brothers, and sisters attended. I was disappointed that my father, who had been killed in a work-related accident during my junior year, could not be there to watch me receive my diploma.

My mother was so proud. It was her dream to see me graduate since I was her youngest and the first of her children to do so. Being the youngest child in my family, my brothers and sisters often teased me and accused me of being spoiled. That may have been true. I know I had it better than them because they grew up in the aftermath of the Depression and had to go to work before they could finish high school. I was my mother's "baby," and I was happy I could fulfill her dream.

Chapter 3

Deferring College Football

During recruiting season in the spring of 1956, I visited several universities, but I knew I was going to Ohio State. I was seventeen years old when I graduated in June 1956. On August 12, I turned eighteen. Around the middle of August, I was off to The Ohio State University to play for Woody Hayes. I was very proud to be a Buckeye.

Freshmen, then, were ineligible to play varsity football, so they were basically the scout team who ran the opponent's offense and defense. We got beaten up every day, but I enjoyed competing and had a very good freshman season.

The freshman coach, Clive Rush, believed in the passing game a bit more than Woody, so when we played freshman games away from home, I got the opportunity to catch the ball. On the other hand, Woody believed in the "three yards and a cloud of dust" philosophy.

In other words, run, run, run—and that was OK. At Ohio State, receivers were blockers first, and, at 162 pounds, I knew I would not be an effective blocker in the Big Ten Conference. OSU receivers were lucky to have two passes thrown their way in a game until Paul Warfield—who earned a Hall of Fame NFL career with the Cleveland Browns and Miami Dolphins as a wide receiver—changed Woody's thinking just a bit when he enrolled in 1958.

I knew my college football career options would be limited at OSU. Even though I was a good receiver, I was no Paul Warfield. I knew I would have a better chance to play at The University of Akron, so I transferred there at the end of the fall semester. Fortunately, I was in good academic standing. The OSU coaches tried to persuade me to stay, but I had decided it was best for me to leave.

When I returned home to Akron, things had changed. Spending time on a college campus helped me mature and changed my perspective. Hanging out with my boys at home was not the same. I got a part-time job, hung out in the pool room, and played basketball at the community center.

Although all of my friends had graduated from high school, I was the only one who spent any time in college. Their lives had not dramatically changed. They were doing the same things we did in high school. Many of them worked in the factories. Some had tried boxing because Gordon Dokes, who played football at South several years before me, was a heavyweight who was nationally ranked.

Out of boredom, I started going to the boxing gym and found that I had some natural skills. I had quick hands and I was hard to hit, which is a good thing for a boxer. At 169 pounds, I was very quick and had good foot movement, probably because of my football training. As a youngster, I had been in many fistfights—not because I liked to fight, but to survive. In our neighborhood, I had to show no fear and defend myself. I never considered myself a tough guy, but I was tough enough to gain respect.

When the time rolled around for the Akron Golden Gloves Tournament, I was one of two light heavyweights from our gym. If we both kept winning, we would eventually fight each other. With that in mind, I stayed away from him in the gym because I did not want to befriend someone I might have to beat up. We both won our first match and were scheduled to fight each other in the second match.

At the time, I did not understand the term *killer instinct*, but that fight taught me what it meant. I define it as wanting to destroy whoever or whatever is in your path. You transform yourself into another person—almost like a Jekyll and Hyde moment. It was just like football. When the fight began, I went after him as if it were the last time I would ever fight. For the first time, I saw fear in a man's eyes. He made it through the first round, but early in the second, the referee stopped the fight. I advanced to the championship fight.

In the championship fight, it seemed all of South Akron was in the Akron Armory. My opponent was Benny Calhoun from West Akron. On the streets, everybody knew Benny was someone you did not want to mess with. He was tough and an outstanding halfback for West High School.

Benny was short, muscular, and deaf. When we got into the ring the referee told me he would come between us at the bell and that we should protect ourselves at all times. When the fight started, Benny charged at me, swinging both fists. I used my speed to avoid his charges and jabbed him from the outside. I was in control of the fight until the bell rang. I had forgotten, and evidently so had the referee, about Benny's disability. Benny could not hear the bell. Just as I relaxed to return to my corner, I saw Benny charging but could not avoid him hitting me with an overhand right. The blood squirted out of my nose, and Benny continued attacking until the corner men rushed out. I was not hurt, but I had never been angrier. During that minute's rest, I decided that if he wanted a brawl that was what he was going to get.

He came out in the second round just as he had the first—charging and swinging. This time I did not move away. When he threw a round-house right, I ducked, planted and hit him with a left hook to the side of his head followed by a straight right to the solar plexus. When the right landed, it appeared as though he was paralyzed. His put up his hands and stared at me, but he just stood there.

I went for the kill. I don't know how many punches I threw before the referee stopped the fight. I had won the tournament. My brother Chester told me later that Benny came to my corner and apologized for hitting me after the bell, but I must have still been in that moment because I did not see or hear him.

That bout propelled me to the State Golden Gloves Championships in Cleveland. I won my fight in the semifinals and advanced to the championship fight. My opponent was a fighter from Canton, Ohio. To this day I remember his name—Paul Denunzio. We sat side-by-side in the waiting area and although the weight limit was 175, he seemed a lot bigger. Looking at his physical structure, I decided he would be a plodder looking for an opportunity to throw a big punch.

I mapped out my game plan. In the first two rounds, I "out-quicked" him and hit him regularly. Paul was strong but slow. He kept plodding forward and I evaded him and landed a bunch of blows without taking many. After the first two rounds, his face was red and his nose was bloody; he looked worse than Joe Frazier in Muhammad Ali's comeback fight. In the third round, I got tired and tried to elude him. However, unlike the first two rounds, my legs wouldn't allow me to dance out of his persistent forward charges. I tried to hold on and ride it out, but he kept coming. He won the third round convincingly—my own fault—and I ran out of gas.

My coaches told me that I did not fight like I wanted to be a champion because champions fight to the very end. I had sabotaged my own effort by not training hard enough. I fought in a couple more club fights that I won at the Akron Armory before giving up boxing. However, that third round in Cleveland remained with me. From then on, when I competed as a player or as a coach I always prepared—mentally and physically—for all contingencies.

In the aftermath of my last fight, I realized I had to do more with my life than just hang out. The guys I had grown up with were still my boys, but they were happy with jobs in the rubber factories. I wanted more. I still had my mind set on returning to Ohio State, but I knew that ship had sailed.

While playing football at South High School, I never considered playing for The University of Akron. In fact, I had never been to a sporting event at the university. The athletic program there was, at best, mediocre except for the basketball and soccer teams. So, in early March 1957, I decided to join the Army Reserves.

On April 6, 1957, I boarded a Greyhound bus to Fort Knox, Kentucky, to report for basic training. It was my first trip South as an adult. I had some reservations because my mother had told me some scary stories about the treatment of "colored" people in the South. I knew about the Emmett Till murder in Mississippi. However, what she had told me did not make much of an impact until I made that bus trip to Kentucky. We had about a ninety-minute layover in Louisville, so I decided to walk around the terminal. I stopped to take a drink of water and I heard a booming voice say, "Hey boy, what do you think you're doing?"

I turned around to see who was speaking. The officer must have thought I was being a smart-ass because he said, "I'm talking to you niggah!"

I knew I had not done anything wrong, so I asked him, "What's the problem, officer?"

"Can't you read?"

"Yeah!"

"Well, look at the damn sign above the fountain!"

I looked. The sign read, "Whites." Next to it, at the other fountain, the sign said, "Colored."

"You're drinking at the wrong fountain, boy. Where you from, boy?" He seemed to like the word "boy."

I replied, "Akron, Ohio. I'm on my way to report for duty at Fort Knox."

"Well, you ain't in Akron, O-Hi-O now boy! You better learn how we do things down heah!"

That experience remains etched in my memory to this day. It would not be the last experience of that type that I would have while in Kentucky.

After completing basic training at Fort Knox, I was stationed at Camp Breckenridge, Kentucky. One Saturday evening, several of us went into Morganfield, a small town eight or nine miles from the post. After surveying the town for a while, we decided to go to a movie. There were five of us—four blacks and Bobby DeVega, a Latino from New York.

We went to the ticket office to purchase tickets. The women in the office told us to go upstairs to the balcony. We were in uniform and I thought they were letting soldiers in free of charge. When we reached the balcony, all we saw were black people. The light bulb went off—these were the segregated seats. We stood there for a moment and then I said, "Let's go downstairs!"

On the way down we passed an usher on his way upstairs to collect the money for admission from the black patrons. When we reached the sidewalk, we entered the main entrance to the theater and found seats about midway down the aisle. Less than five minutes after we sat down, there was a loud noise behind us as six policemen rushed in, hands on guns, and stationed themselves on both ends of the row we were sitting in. They motioned for us to get up and stand in the aisle. When we did they surrounded us, hands still on guns, and marched us up the aisle, out the door, and into a van that took us directly to jail.

Nearly two hours after our detention—the police told us we were not under arrest—the military police from the base showed up and we were released. It was a short ride back to the post and when we arrived at the sergeant's office, he was standing there smoking a cigarette, waiting for us. I recalled my mother standing on the porch when Archie and Craig brought me home.

We entered the office and, before we could sit down, First Sergeant Don Melnick blurted out, "What the hell do you young soldiers think you are doing?" He did not expect an answer, and we said nothing.

He went on: "They said you forced your way into the theater without paying. Is that true?" This time he expected an answer. I told him what had happened, and I could tell by his body language that he understood. I finished by saying that we were soldiers who might be called on to die for this country. Why should we be treated like we are not good enough to sit any place in the theater? He had been standing the whole time, but now, he went behind his desk and sat down.

"Take a seat, soldiers!" He told us that even though he did not agree with segregation, we weren't here to change Kentucky traditions. In the future, we would follow the customs of the communities around the base—"and that is an order!" He then dismissed us. The "ass-chewing" had not been as bad as I thought it would be, but it was disappointing.

This incident took place on Saturday. On the following Wednesday, a directive was posted on the company bulletin board. It read:

"Effective immediately, the Morganfield theater is off-limits to all personnel at Camp Breckenridge."

Several weeks later, the directive was lifted. Apparently more than half of the theater's patrons were soldiers. They faced going out of business or relenting on their seating policy. They chose the latter. Just like that, segregation in the Morganfield Theater ended. Go Army!

In the Army, we were told what time to eat, go to bed, get up, and even take latrine breaks. We did what we were told even if there was a better way of accomplishing a task.

There are three ways of doing things—the right way, the wrong way, and the army way. The army way always takes precedence. I now understand the reasons for this type of structure. However, I decided that I needed to find a way to have more say-so in my life. A college education became absolutely necessary.

I was a good soldier. I earned soldier of the month and became a squad leader during basic training. Becoming a squad leader was no big deal. I got the job because I opened my mouth when the sergeant asked whether anyone had any military experience and said I had been in ROTC.

Without any opposition, I got the job of leading the fourth squad. The guys in my squad were always trying to show their manliness and that caused me problems. An old adage in the Army is, "sh——t" runs downhill. So, when they screwed up, the sergeant chewed me out. So, I got tough on them. Being thrust into leadership helped me because it became my responsibility to help them become a cohesive, disciplined unit.

Every day I was putting out fires. But little by little, they began to whip themselves into shape. At the end of basic training, the fourth platoon received several commendations, and I was selected top platoon leader.

While stationed at Camp Breckenridge, the United States was involved in the Vietnam War. In early September 1957, our battalion was put on alert and I thought we were going to be shipped out to Vietnam. I had a lot of time to think while we sat on the airstrip for twelve hours before being ordered back to quarters. My most prominent thoughts revolved around the reality that there would be men trying to kill me and I might have to kill another person. That reality seemed insane to me and still does. Wars kill our youngest, best, and brightest. I thought of my mother, the rest of my family, and how I wanted to live a long, productive life. If I made it back home, I would make every effort to do just that.

After completing my active duty, I was released on October 7, 1957, to begin completing the rest of my seven-and-a-half years in the Reserves.

Upon returning home, I enrolled at The University of Akron for the spring semester of 1958. I then went to see Joe McMullen, the head football coach, to learn whether any football scholarships were available. He had tried to recruit me out of high school but gave up when I told him I was going to Ohio State.

There were no scholarships available, but he told me that I could walk on and possibly earn a scholarship if I made first or second team. I knew that if I got a fair opportunity, I would make the team. This was not arrogance; having competed in high school against many of the athletes on the team, I knew I was a better player than most of them.

I enrolled that spring.

*

College for me was not all about football. Like most students, I partied and had a good time. My short time in the service had matured me somewhat more than my friends who had stayed home and were now attending The University of Akron. Nevertheless, I had a tough time academically during my first year. In high school, I was counseled to take the General Course of Studies that included General Math, Business Training, etc. rather than Algebra, Geometry, and the rest of the college curriculum. History was my best subject; it was interesting to me and I really liked Mrs. Hall, our history teacher, so I did very well.

Even though I had spent a quarter at Ohio State, I was not ready for college. That fact became abundantly clear during my first day in English class. The professor, Dr. Keister, presented an overview of the class requirements, which included book reports and research papers. I had not done either in high school. Somehow the discussion turned to William Shakespeare, a man of whom I had no knowledge. Several students joined the lively discussion and one of them even knew when he was born (1564). I thought to myself—damn, where did these people come from? I was the only black student in the class, and I sat there hoping he would not ask me anything. He did not and when the bell rang, I quickly made my way to the door and escaped to the hallway.

Reasoning and Understanding Science was my next class. It was a lecture class with more than one hundred and fifty students. Dr. Sumner, the lecturer, gave a few opening remarks and then dropped a bomb. He told us to look at the students to the left and right of us. When we did, he said those two students will not be here at the end of the semester. Those two classes messed up my whole day. The only science I had taken was biology. Dr. Sumner spoke about studying Galileo, genes, heredity, and several other subjects I had never heard of. I was definitely out of my lane and in some deep sh——t!

Those two classes at nine and ten o'clock were my only classes on Monday-Wednesday-Friday. I went back to my dorm after the Science class and reviewed my notes. After about an hour, I headed to the library to read the assigned chapters and study. I did not leave the library until 2:45. I had forgotten all about lunch. I spent many hours outside of class playing catch-up trying to learn things I should have learned in high school.

Dr. Keister didn't help my confidence when he called me to his office after I received an F on my first theme paper in his class. There was more red marking on the paper than black. He was sitting behind his desk peering at me over his glasses.

"Mr. Greene," he said, "after reviewing your paper, I don't see how you are going to be successful at this university." I had expected some help and his words crushed me. He went on, "I don't want to sound harsh, but you are going to have a difficult time."

What could I say? I finally told him that I would work harder and left his office. While devastated at the time, I did study and work harder. I ended up getting a C- in his class and a D in science. That was the only D I received for the rest of my college career. I had Dr. Keister for a couple more classes as a sophomore and junior and I earned Bs. Passing him one day in the Fine Arts Building, he stopped me and told me he was pleasantly surprised at how much I had improved. I looked him in the eye, shook his hand and thanked him.

There was no spring practice then, so I took classes and worked out on my own from January through the summer. While on campus, I met several members of the football team and learned as much as I could about Akron's offense and defense in preparation for fall practice.

When practice began in August 1958, I was the fastest among the receivers and defensive backs on the team. Our team did not have the physical stature or talent of the players at Ohio State, but we had some good athletes. I reported in good physical condition and was physically and mentally prepared for any of the agility and strength tests they put us through. The rules then required playing offense, defense, and special teams.

Coach McMullen was a big man. He was not necessarily well built or muscular. He was just big. He wore a large, white cowboy hat on his huge head every day. Some of the players fondly referred to him as "bucket head." For others, the nickname was less than complimentary. Regardless, it was an accurate description.

McMullen was an electrical engineer by training and a very smart guy. When he came into the room for our first team meeting, he put his hat on the table, introduced the staff and began telling us what to expect. It was the normal talk that coaches give—nothing special.

When he finished with the administrative speech, he uncovered the big board behind him containing the depth chart from the previous fall plus the walk-ons. I looked for my name and was completely surprised, although I should not have been, when I saw it at the bottom of the list of receivers. It was the same on the defensive board where I was the fourth, and last, defensive back listed on the right side.

I was disappointed but not discouraged. I knew that given a fair opportunity, I would move up. However, not everything was fair. During the first four days of practice, I had few opportunities to move up on the depth chart. I paid attention in meetings and understood the offensive and defensive schemes, but my role in practice was relegated to holding the blocking bags as a scout team member.

I went through all of the drills; that gave me an opportunity to show my athletic ability, but I never got an opportunity to run plays or play on defense or offense with the first or second teams. This was, I believe, because Coach McMullen decided who he wanted to participate and I, evidently, was not in his plans.

On the fifth day of practice, an afternoon scrimmage was scheduled. I thought this would be my opportunity. However, after the morning practice, several players and I were told to go to campus to register for classes. We ate lunch and headed to register at about twelve-thirty.

Upon arriving to register, we had to stand in line for about ninety minutes before beginning the process. The afternoon practice started at three. I worried about being late and missing my chance to scrimmage. Finally, at five minutes to three, I finished. The rest of the guys did not finish until 3:20.

When they finished, we ran to the car and rushed to the practice complex. There were four of us and we could see the team on the field going through preliminary drills leading up to the scrimmage. One of my teammates said, we don't have to go out because they know we are registering for classes. I told them they could stay, but I was going out. It was one of the best decisions I have ever made.

I hurriedly got dressed and ran onto the field. I finished a brief warm-up and went down to the end where they had begun the scrimmage. Coach Andy Maluke, the defensive coordinator, who had been encouraging me throughout the week, called out, "Greene, get in here at defensive end!" I hadn't played defensive end since high school, but it was an opportunity, so I complied.

The defensive scout team went against the first-team offense as cannon fodder. On the first play, they ran a toss sweep to my side. I beat the block and made the tackle for a five-yard loss. On the second play, they ran the sweep to the other side. I chased the play down from behind and made another tackle for a loss. The offensive coaches were getting very upset. Someone yelled, "Can somebody block number 80?"

I was relegated to a number. The killer instinct kicked in. I yelled out, "No, they can't block me!" I really did not remember saying it, but my boys told me that I did.

For the next five consecutive plays, they ran at me. I made every play. Coach Maluke came over to congratulate me. "Good job, Ray! Now, take a blow."

The next morning, when I went into the locker room, I noticed someone had put an apple, an orange, and a Hershey bar in my locker. Lying beside these items was a new pair of socks, a jock strap, a T-shirt, and shorts. I went to our equipment man, "Porky" Dudich, to ask him who put them there.

Porky answered in his squeaky, whining voice, "I did!" It was Porky's tradition to reward players who made the squad. I asked him how he knew I had made the team. "I know everything that goes on around here. Go take a look at the depth chart."

My years in coaching have taught me that equipment men and trainers really do know everything that happens around the team and coaches.

I rushed into the meeting room to look at the depth chart. I did not see my name at all under the defensive backs. As I scanned the board, I found my name listed No. 2 at left defensive end. I had made the first step toward being a starter.

After our offensive position meeting, I asked Coach Tony Laterza, the receiver's coach, when was I going to get an opportunity to move up the offensive depth chart. He told me I could move up when I proved I could block and catch the ball.

I looked right at him. "Coach, I can do both if you give me the opportunity." During our next full scrimmage that Saturday, I caught five passes, including one for a touchdown, and made several key blocks. I had a good overall performance. I ultimately moved up to No. 2 at wide receiver, as well as defensive end. I felt confident as we began to prepare for game week.

I did not get into the first game until late in the second quarter. We were on defense. The offense called a pass on the first play and the running back was assigned to block me. I eluded him easily, sacked the quarterback, and forced him to fumble the ball.

At the end of the game, I had recorded 3.5 sacks and made seven tackles. On offense, I caught the only pass thrown my way and blocked adequately. I started every game after that. I should have started every game for the next two seasons, but in the middle of 1960, I got in Coach McMullen's doghouse.

In 1959, the NCAA instituted the new two-platoon system. We had to play both ways and on special teams. The rules dictated that a player could be substituted twice in a quarter. Here is the scenario: if we got the ball first, Jim Lupori started and played until the offense scored or punted. At that point, I would go in on defense. After two possessions and substitutions on offense or defense, either Jim or I would have to play both ways until the end of the quarter. Because of the substitution rule, I got the opportunity to play on offense for the first time and caught my first pass in a collegiate game.

In 1959 I was named honorable mention on the All-Ohio Conference team and looked forward to our team having a better than 4–5 record the next fall. That did not work out the way I had planned.

We were not a good football team in 1960. In our first four games, our record was 0–4. Three of these games we lost by the identical score of 27–0. This start made Coach McMullen very angry. Instead of trying to motivate, he became derisive and, for all intents and purposes, he lost control of the team.

The team had pretty much given up and was just going through the motions. Personally, I was having a good season. Our offense was ineffective, so we played a lot of defense. I was leading the league in sacks and tackles-for-losses and had been good on special teams, especially covering punts. We punted a lot.

One day in the locker room after practice, Coach McMullen overheard part of a conversation I was having with several teammates. There were only four black guys on the team, and it was common for players to discuss racial issues. Some of the white players didn't have much interaction with black people and welcomed insight into how we thought about various issues. This particular day we were discussing a controversy involving Paul Brown, the head coach of the Cleveland Browns and Bobby Mitchell, who started at running back with Jim Brown. At the time Jim Brown and Bobby Mitchell were one and two in rushing in the NFL. The newspapers reported that Bobby had said he should be getting more carries. Paul Brown started benching him more and more. I loved Jim Brown, but I agreed with Bobby. He was probably the most exciting player in the league. Jim Brown ran straight ahead, but Bobby made people miss and ran like he had eyes in the back of his head. People loved Jim Brown, but they wanted to see Bobby Mitchell. At the end of the season, Paul Brown traded him to the Washington Redskins and he had a Hall-of-Fame career with Washington as a wide receiver.

I told the players in the locker room that I thought Paul Brown did not like the idea of anyone questioning his judgment, especially a colored player. The coach burst into the room, exclaiming that "him being colored had nothing to do with it!" He looked directly at me even though several other players had expressed the same thought. I said nothing. He asked me why I thought that and I replied, "Coach, it's just my opinion."

He looked at me. "It's a good thing that your opinion doesn't matter." He walked out.

Friction was growing between us.

The friction increased when Ken MacDonald wrote a complimentary article about me in the university's newspaper, *The Buchtelite*. In the two-platoon system, I mostly played defense. However, I did catch nine passes that season. After our third 27–0 loss, Ken MacDonald, the student sports editor of the campus paper, wrote that Baldwin Wallace's coach, Lee Tressell, the father of former Ohio State coach Jim Tressell, said I was, without a doubt, the best defensive end in the conference. Though I appreciated the comment, it did not make up for the disappointing season we were having as a team.

On Tuesday, the day after the paper came out, Coach McMullen called me to his office. When I knocked on the door and entered, he threw the paper down on his desk in front of me and asked whether I had thought I deserved this praise in the article.

Still standing, I said, "Coach, I didn't write the article."

He repeated, "Do you think you deserve this?"

I was unsure how to respond. I told him that Coach Laterza, my receiver coach, gave me a grade of 88% on my performance. I made several big plays and had a couple of sacks. His reply was, "George Grosso made more plays than you." George Grosso was the defensive end on the other side.

I concealed my rising anger as best as I could. I couldn't say what I was really thinking, which was "Hell, they stopped running at me when they found that they couldn't." Sometimes, remaining silent is the best course of action. Besides, he had seen the film and knew I had had a good game. I am sure he felt my anger, so he dismissed me and I left.

For the rest of the season, I played sparingly. Still, I made the All-Conference first team. That must have really pissed him off. I tried to keep a good attitude, but evidently Coach Maluke noticed how I really felt. He approached me after practice one afternoon and told me he wanted to speak with me. The next morning, I went to his office. After a few pleasantries, he told me that my feelings were reflected in the way I was practicing. He also said he didn't agree with me being benched and went on to give me some valuable advice that helped me navigate through my disappointment: "We all have disappointments, but we can't let them define who we are; we are defined by how we overcome them and continue to work toward our objectives. What are your objectives, Ray?"

I thought for a while and said my immediate objectives were to be the best player I could be and to graduate from college. He said that being the best player I could be depended on how I handled this situation going forward. "Don't let anyone get in your head to the point that it affects your ability as a player," he said. I left his office feeling as though a heavy burden had been lifted.

McMullen was fired right after the season, and my first high school coach, Gordon Larson, was hired.

*

Several years before Coach Larson coached at The University of Akron, he worked at Marion Harding High School, one of the powerhouse football schools in southern Ohio. He turned things around his first year. After two years at Marion, he had the team ranked among the top ten teams in Ohio. He then left Marion to accept a position at Ohio State, where he coached with Woody Hayes for two seasons before coming to The University of Akron.

Shortly after his arrival, Coach Larson called me to his office. I took the opportunity to ask him what I had wondered about since he cut me from the football team many years before. I said, "Coach, do you remember when you dismissed me from the team when I was a freshman?"

He looked at me for a while, I guess, trying to remember. "Yes, I remember. You were late for practice." He asked me why I wanted to know.

I told him I wanted to know if he would have dismissed me if he knew the kind of ability I had and the kind of player I could become. He answered, "No, I don't think I would have!"

I always respected him as a man, but his response enhanced that. I think of that moment each time a player asks me a direct question. I always answer directly and truthfully no matter the circumstance. Some have not liked my directness; however, several of those, years after they graduated, have come back to tell me how much they appreciated it.

There were four former South High players on Akron's team, and we were elated that Larson was going to be our coach again. About a week after he was hired and settled in his office, Coach Larson started interviewing players. When my time came, I went into his office and he greeted me warmly. After a little small talk about old times, he asked me why he did not see me on film the last two games of the season. I believe he had already spoken with Coach Maluke and just wanted to hear my side.

I told my side of the story and reassured him that the drama was in the past. I also let him know he could depend on me to provide the senior leadership that we lacked last season. He told me he would. I left his office with a good feeling.

We were all excited about the coming season. We had some talented players on the team and Larson brought in more during the spring. When fall practice began, the starting lineup was mostly seniors. His system was nearly the same as the one he used at South High, so we South guys were somewhat familiar with it. Larson was a stickler for details, and our practices were organized and spirited.

He always posted a practice schedule and it was strictly followed. He told us that when the horn sounded, ending practice, everything stopped.

If we were in the middle of running a play, it stopped. I followed this same practice when I became a head coach. With McMullen, we never knew when practice was going to end. There was always one more play he wanted to run. As a result, many players didn't go all out on every play, anticipating that practice would never end on time. Larson changed that. We knew when practice would be over and we went all out until the horn sounded.

When the season began, we were ready. We lost the first game, 7–0, against Wittenberg, an Ohio Conference powerhouse, but we played much better than most people expected. We then won four straight games before losing to Baldwin-Wallace, 7–0. In that loss, we made dumb mistakes that every losing team makes—turnovers, missed tackles, missed assignments, dropped passes, etc. When we got back to practice, as a team we pledged to never to play that way again.

We won our remaining games and finished second in the conference—quite a turnaround from the previous season. Many of my teammates received postseason honors. I was named to the All-Conference and Small College All-America teams.

In the process, comparing the previous two seasons, I learned a lot about steps necessary to be a successful coach: organization, senior leadership, and stressing technique. What I learned from Coach Larson and his assistants served me well when I started coaching. Coach Maluke's advice on handling disappointments also had a great impact on my coaching philosophy.

Upon finishing my playing eligibility at the university, I was ten hours short of the credits I needed to graduate. I went to Coach Larson to ask if there was any way I could help the team while completing my graduation requirements. He asked me if I wanted to help coach, which surprised me. I had never thought seriously about coaching, but I needed the money and credits to finish school. I agreed. I became the first "official" graduate assistant on the football team at The University of Akron. Additionally, I became the first black person to coach any sport at the university.

I was the first black coach at Kenmore High School, The University of Akron, the University of Miami in Florida, and Iowa State University. Each of those schools have photos of all of their teams and coaches that date back to when they began playing sports, and I never saw a black coach on any of the staff pictures, except at Iowa State. Bobby Douglas, who is black, was an assistant coach on the ISU wrestling team when I arrived there in 1969. Bobby went on to have a great career as a head coach at Temple.

When I took the graduate assistant job at Akron, it never crossed my mind that I was their first black coach, so I never thought of it as a big deal.

When the next season began, I was basically a gofer for the coaches. Anything that the coaches did not want to do became my job. When practice started, I was assigned to work with wide receivers and defensive ends. Although most of the players were guys I had played with, they paid attention and listened to me. I had earned their respect as a player and, after a few days, they started calling me "Coach." I told them to call me Ray, but they continued to call me "Coach." I had made the transition from teammate to coach.

I sat in coaches' meetings and absorbed everything I could because I was beginning to like the idea of being a coach. I loved the game. When we began practice for game week, Coach Larson told me he wanted me in the press box.

I was a little disappointed because my ego wanted me to be on the sideline so my friends and family could see me. After all, I was the only black football coach in the city of Akron. I thought I was being exiled to the press box so I would not get in the way of the other coaches on the sideline.

Later, Coach Larson, who must have sensed my displeasure about my game-day assignment, took me aside and told me, "Ray, I put you in the press box because I trust your judgment and have been impressed with the work you put in to learn our entire offense, defense, and kicking game schemes." I was elated and my initial disappointment was replaced with a new sense of pride. It was also a step in developing a philosophy that I believed then and now. If you work hard, success will come because somebody is always watching and will reward hard work.

The freshman team at Akron played their games on Mondays. Coach Larson called me into his office on Monday morning and told me that Coach Dick Wright would be the head freshman coach. However, he wanted me to run the team. Dick's primary job was swimming coach, but he was assigned the freshman football job to help justify his salary. He had not played football and knew little about the game. Larson told me that Dick understood the arrangement. I spoke to Dick to try to avoid any friction between us in case there was some resentment. Dick told me the arrangement was fine with him and that he would take care of all the administrative duties and let me take care of the coaching.

Just like that, I was now a head football coach. That season, we won four, lost one, and tied one. (There was no overtime then.) I made mistakes, including one that contributed to our only loss, but it was a great learning experience. I developed this philosophy: if you have a play that is working for you, run it until the defense stops it. If they stop it a few times, run it some more just to make sure they have not figured it out.

I have watched hundreds of football games, and it is surprising to watch coaches stop running a successful play because they believe the defense has learned to stop it. When they look at the tapes, they figuratively kick themselves because they learn that the defense had not stopped it. The play was actually stopped because of the offense's mental or physical errors.

Still, they don't learn. They do the very same thing the following week. Coaches in the press box are supposed to let the play callers on the sideline know what is happening on the field. Unfortunately, some coaches on the sideline put coaches in the press box just so they will not be in the way on the sideline. (Thank you, Coach Larson, for the real opportunity you gave me.)

Larson put me in the press box because he trusted my ability to assess what was happening and suggest adjustments at halftime.

After completing college, I would have loved being drafted by the NFL but, truthfully, I knew I was not good enough. I signed a free agent contract with the Minnesota Vikings. They were impressed that I had played offense, defense, and special teams in college. I became a member of what they then called the "taxi squad." That meant that if someone got hurt, because of my versatility, I could temporarily fill a roster spot until the injured player was able to play again. Unfortunately for me, but fortunately for the Vikings, no one got hurt.

I lasted through the preseason and the first three games of the regular season before I was released. I needed to get a real job.

GRADUATION

I graduated Akron in the spring of 1963 and after my brief stint in professional football, I began looking for a job. I put my teaching certificate on file with the Akron Public Schools but heard nothing all summer. In August, just before the start of high school football practice, I went to see Bill Hawkins, the head football coach at South High School. I offered to volunteer to help coach until the season started and coached at South for a few weeks.

It was getting close to the start of school when a friend in Cleveland called to tell me the Cleveland system was hiring teachers. That was great news. I didn't have a car so the next day, I boarded a Greyhound bus for the twenty-eight-mile trip to Cleveland. I took a cab to the Board of Education office, interviewed, and was told on the spot that I had a job teaching special education. It was not my field, so I would need to take some night classes toward certification and mail them my teaching certificate that was on file in Akron.

When I got back to Akron, my first stop was the Akron Board of Education to retrieve my teaching certificate. On the way out of the building, I ran into Larry Dessart, the Director of Athletics for the city's schools. When I told him why I was there, he replied that they were working on getting me a position in Akron. I held my composure and informed him that I had already committed to a job in Cleveland. Leaving the building, I felt I had been screwed around.

Approximately three hours after arriving home, I received a call from George Boss, a local businessman and big supporter of University of Akron football. Mr. Boss asked me to meet him for lunch the next day at the University Club.

I doubt whether a black person had ever had lunch at the club, and I knew there were no black members because there had been some controversy about that a while back in the *Akron Beacon Journal*. I arrived on time. The hostess told me they were expecting me and that Mr. Boss was waiting in the dining room. She had no trouble recognizing me. When I got to the table, Mr. Boss was sitting there talking with Larry Dessart. They greeted me and invited me to sit down.

Mr. Boss was a short man with a friendly, reddish face and a soft, gravelly voice. He began by asking me whether I would be interested in staying home to coach if he could assist me in getting a teaching position.

I told him I would but that I had already committed to go to Cleveland and I did not want to break my word. He assured me that he understood and that me he could handle the situation so I would not lose any future opportunities if I decided to apply in Cleveland at a later date.

He was a man I believed I could trust. He went on to say that he knew I wanted to coach at South High School, but there was no opening there. "If you want to stay here, you will have to coach at Kenmore High School." He told me I would be teaching physical education at Lane Elementary, where Mr. Miller from the community center was principal. He also assured me that if a teaching position opened at Kenmore, I would be hired there the next year. He was true to his word. My second year in the system I was hired at Kenmore to teach speech and physical education.

Chapter 4

Kenmore High School, Home of the Fighting Cardinals
First High School Coaching Position

In September 1963, I was hired to teach at Lane Elementary and coach at Kenmore High. Kenmore, a blue-collar suburb of Akron, was just about all white. At South, we referred to them as the "Friendly Cardinals." They had a lot of players on the team who were not averse to taking cheap shots or using the N-word during our games. For us at South, their toughness off the field was lacking when they played football. Kenmore was always a sure win.

They were not a very tough or physical team and South could usually score as many points as we wanted when we played them. It was almost like a practice scrimmage. I was Kenmore's offensive assistant coach—the only black coach in the city and the only black teacher at Lane school even though Mr. Miller, the principal, was black. I was coaching a team I did not like, in an environment I did not want to be in.

I didn't know anyone on the coaching staff. They knew me because they followed South and Zips football. I expected some resistance from them because they had no say in my selection. However, I felt no animosity and they were surprisingly friendly. The head coach, Dick Fortner, was also new. I found him to be a good football man and thoughtful person. He was organized and had a great plan to turn the program around.

When I first met our players, I noticed that there was only one black athlete in the room, Herman Smith. When Coach Fortner introduced me, the players stood and applauded—a really classy move. Later, I learned that Fortner instituted this practice when he introduced any teacher or other adult to the team. I emulated that practice throughout my coaching career. Most people are impressed with a standing ovation because few ever get one.

As I looked around the room, I knew there was a lot of work to do. These guys did not look like the ones at South in hue or body structure. There were a few rangy-looking athletes, but none were physically imposing. I thought we would be lucky to win one game.

Still, it was obvious to me that they were a close team in spite of their lack of success in football. The team totally accepted Herman, which was a good sign. After getting to know him, I understood why. He was a bright, personable young man who did not have a selfish bone in his body, despite being a track star and an otherwise outstanding athlete.

The fall before I got there, the team had won two of nine games and only three games in the last four years. Their wins came mostly against county teams in a lower classification, but winning is winning. Their progress caused everyone to be excited about the coming season.

During the spring of that year, the staff went to the Ohio All-Star game and football clinic in Canton, Ohio, the home of the Pro Football Hall of Fame. One of the coaches in that game was Glenn "Tiger" Ellison. He was a very successful head coach at Middletown High School in southern Ohio. After several mediocre seasons, he invented the "Lonesome Polecat Offense," which would later evolve to become the "Run and Shoot" and then "The Spread."

Tiger put that offense into a book, *Run and Shoot Football: Offense of the Future.* The offense boils down to using four wide receivers, running motion on every play, making every pass look like a run and every run look like a pass, throwing on any down from any place on the field, taking the easy throw, and having fun. He gave his quarterback the option to check off any play from the line. Even Paul Brown, the legendary coach of the NFL's Cleveland Browns, didn't allow his quarterbacks to check off, so this was a pretty big deal for our players.

Our staff cornered Tiger in the lobby of the Onesta Hotel one morning between practices and began questioning him about his new offense. In his excitement about his offense, we talked for almost three hours. We bought six copies that were on sale at the hotel. I still have mine. Coach Fortner was sold on Tiger's idea and told us that we would be running the Run and Shoot that fall, which suited me just fine.

Meanwhile, back at Kenmore, I learned quickly that looks can be deceiving. The group impressed me in practice with their good speed and grit. They were small but quick and had a couple of very fine athletes, especially at the quarterback and receiver positions.

Summer practice paid off. We had a good weight program, and the quarterbacks and receivers spent a lot of time throwing and catching footballs. Some coaches in the city accused us of having summer football practice because every time they drove by our practice field, nearly our whole team was there working out. Coach Fortner petitioned and received approval from the Ohio High School Athletic Association to conduct our summer workout program so their complaints were without foundation. While the other coaches in the city took the summer off, our staff was working to get our players bigger, stronger, and faster.

Other activities with our athletes brought us closer as a team. We had picnics, took them to movies, church, and visited their families. Many coaches speak about their team being a family. Coach Fortner, the architect of this process, had created something that Kenmore never had—pride in a team. Everyone cared about each other. I continued to use his ideas throughout my coaching career.

Another brilliant idea of Coach Fortner's was for coaches to visit the homes of those we coached (quarterbacks and receivers, in my case). The objective was to let the parents know what we expected from their sons and the importance of them assisting us off the field. From those visits, the parents formed a group that supported us throughout the season. Fortner always looked at the big picture and involved as many people as possible in the program—a valuable asset for a head coach.

Our quarterback, Sonny Litz, was an outstanding player who received an appointment to the Air Force Academy after his senior season. Ronnie Miller, at 6'1", 215 pounds, was a monster at wide receiver. He had great hands and excellent speed. Herman Smith, meanwhile, was the fastest guy on the team. He was so shifty that he could make a defender miss him in a hallway. Because our offensive line was small, yet nimble, the Run and

Shoot was a perfect offense. We coached our line to scramble-block (a technique in which the line would come off the ball low, on all fours, and get into the legs of a defender) to compensate for our size disadvantage. The defensive players hated it.

Fortner did not believe in playing the same players on offense and defense, so we divided our team. That meant some of our best players would be sitting when the offense or defense was on the field. The other coaches and I were concerned, but we learned that when players spend 100 percent of their practice time on either offense or defense, they get more repetitions at one position and make fewer mistakes. We also had the luxury of coaching a group of intelligent athletes. They seldom busted assignments and most knew the assignments of the players around them.

When we began the season, no one was ready for our passing offense. We won the first game 52–0 over Ellet and the second game 50–6 over Hower. Our guys gained more confidence with each win. We finished the season 5–2–2. We beat Central in the City Playoffs but lost the Championship to Garfield, 22–0, on Thanksgiving morning in the Rubber Bowl. The crowd of 21,344 people was then the largest ever for an Akron high school football game.

As I progressed as a coach, I gained invaluable knowledge and experience. We had an excellent coaching staff that knew and understood football. They were great teachers who really cared about the young men on the team, and Fortner was an innovator who effectively used psychology to motivate. He would have been a good collegiate coach.

As an example, on the Wednesday before we were to meet Garfield in the playoffs, Fortner yelled, "Stop practice! Look up in the sky!"

We thought he had gone off the deep end. We looked up and saw a group of ducks flying south in a V formation.

"It's a sign from heaven. The V means victory. We're going to win Friday," he said.

Everyone cheered, and the rest of the practice went very well. We coaches knew the V formation had nothing to do with our winning the game; but our players certainly thought it did.

After the season, Fortner left Kenmore to accept another head coaching position. One of our assistants, Gene "Mick" Viland, became head coach. During the summer of 1964, Mick gave me more responsibility. Even though we didn't have an official offensive coordinator, I served in that capacity. I was also the head coach of the junior varsity team. We worked on fitness and strength three days a week for the whole summer. Our guys were in great shape when we began practice. However, because we lost several key players to graduation, we knew we were not going to be as good as we were the previous year.

We won six games but did not make the playoffs. The JV team was comprised mostly of freshmen and went 4–0. I thought I did a good coaching job, but I learned another important lesson: good players are a necessity! The statement, "you can't make chicken salad out of chicken sh——t" is often attributed to Woody Hayes. The longer I coached, the more sense that statement made. To have a great team, you need "chicken salad" athletes.

Coaching the freshmen taught me the value of good athletes. My freshman quarterback, Don Plusquellic, was an outstanding player. He was the Tom Brady type—good looking, intelligent, a natural leader. He could really throw the ball. His arm made me look like a great coach.

Twenty-five years later, I went back to Akron for the holidays and read an article about Mayor Plusquellic. I called his office and confirmed that it was the same guy I had coached in ninth grade. I left a message, and about ten minutes later, Don returned my call. He was on his way to Columbus to meet with the governor.

He told me that playing quarterback was good training for his current position. "When you are the QB, if you win, everybody is with you. When you lose, it's your entire fault. Is that not just like politics?" He said that the most fun he'd ever had playing football was playing on the freshman team at Kenmore. As a coach, I cherish knowing that I had made some difference to him.

In the spring of 1965, a head coaching position became available at Central High School in Akron. I applied for the job.

I thought the job was mine. I had great recommendations both as a teacher and a coach, but they hired a coach whose background did not come close to matching mine. I went to see Larry Dessart, the coordinator of health, physical education, safety, and athletics for the Akron public schools, to learn why I was not selected. He could not give me a definitive answer but said that even though I was given serious consideration, it came down to my lack of coaching experience. In reality, I had more and better coaching experience than the person they hired.

I understood two things from our meeting: first, Mr. Dessart did not want to hire a black head coach and second, the way he spoke to me showed that he still thought of me as the youngster he had taught in elementary school. I resented both and decided to leave the system and find another job.

The following January, in 1966, to everyone's surprise, Mick Viland resigned from Kenmore to take a head coaching job in Fort Pierce, Florida. Mick called me and asked whether I would consider going with him to Florida as his assistant at Dan McCarty High School. They had integrated the school system in Fort Pierce and they wanted him to hire a Negro coach. I told Mick that I would think about it. At the time, I was engaged, and my wedding was to be in July. So, I discussed the matter with my fiancée, Pat, who thought moving to Florida was a great idea. I called Mick and told him I would go. However, I didn't want to make the decision public right away. He agreed.

In early May 1966, Mick told me the Fort Pierce superintendent of schools wanted me to fly to Florida to interview with him. Dr. Vernon Floyd met me at the airport. Dr. Floyd was a Negro who taught at Indian River Junior College. He didn't say much on the short ride from the airport except that some of the Negro residents wanted to meet me that evening at a dinner they had arranged. Dr. Floyd gave me a tour of the town before going to his home, where I was to spend the night.

After meeting his family, he told me I could take a shower and relax before his guests arrived. By 6:30 p.m., there were fifteen to twenty people assembled in his den and on the patio. They were a classy looking group. Introductions were made and there was some small talk before we sat down and consumed a great Southern meal—fried chicken, corn, mashed potatoes, turnip greens, corn bread, and sweet potato pie for dessert. Sitting down to relax after dinner, I learned the real reason I had been brought there. They wanted to size up this Negro from the North.

"Where is your family from?" someone asked.

"Why do you think they hired you, when there are qualified Negro coaches in town?" another asked.

I answered the questions in a straightforward manner. There was no reason not to. Sometimes the questions were humorous, sometimes contentious. I could tell they didn't like all my answers, but the questions kept coming. I had no idea if they could affect my opportunity to get the job, but it didn't matter because I hadn't quit my job back in Akron.

Then, someone asked me about the Civil Rights Movement and what I thought of Bull Connor in Birmingham. I told them that I did not understand how people could allow themselves to be beaten and hosed without fighting back. That answer did not go over well. I thought back to my college days when my friends and I would sit in the Chuckery at The University of Akron and discuss what we would have done in that situation. Later, I realized that fighting back against the beatings and water hoses would have been disastrous.

The crowd went quiet after my answer. Vernon Floyd took a long look at me. "You think you're smarter than Southerners, don't you?"

I thought about my answer for what seemed like a long time. These were movers and shakers in the Negro community. They did not have much say about me getting the job. However, if I accepted the position, they would be the people I would be socializing with. I had never been in a room of all black educated people who were teachers, lawyers, PhDs, and businessmen. I knew I would need their support if I was going to coach here and I didn't want to alienate them. I scanned the room and looked at each person in the room before I spoke.

"You may be right. But, from our discussion this evening, I understand now that I am not. What I learned tonight has helped me uncover my ignorance and I appreciate you taking your time to help me understand." I read their nonverbal reaction to what I had said as forgiveness, of sorts, for my ignorance. There was a little more discussion before everyone started to leave.

The dinner and discussion lasted more than three hours. When everyone left, Vernon and I talked for another hour. He gave me the rundown on what had happened in the city and gave me a heads-up on what to expect from the superintendent of schools, Ben L. Bryant, during my interview the next morning. As a parting note he commented, "You did a good job this evening." I was relieved to hear his assessment and slept soundly.

THE INTERVIEW

Dr. Floyd dropped me off at the superintendent's office and said he would be back in an hour. A young man greeted me at the front door and told me Dr. Bryant would be with me soon. When he came, he greeted me in a Southern drawl. "Good morning, Mr. Greene. I'm Ben L. Bryant!"

Bryant was a short, stocky man. His ruddy face was surrounded by pure white bushy hair. His tie strained to stay close to what little neck he had. He sat behind a big desk that hid his body up to his chest. His drawl made my antenna go up. There was no small talk. He got right to business.

"Mr. Greene, how do you feel about working in a school where the majority of the people are of a different race?" he asked.

I told him that I had been in that type of environment all of my life and that it did not concern me. He went on to tell me that some of the people at the school had allegedly said they would not work with a "niggah." The word flowed easily as though it was part of his everyday vernacular. I quickly understood that he wanted to see how I reacted to his use of the term. I showed no emotion. He was waiting for me to speak.

"Dr. Bryant, I imagine that you have been in many situations where people have said they didn't want to work with you, haven't you? I'll do the best job I can and the rest is on them."

His slight smile grew into a full grin. "Yessuh, son—many, many times!"

He asked about my family and told me that the city did not have any real racial problems. However, he warned, "let me tell you, son, that doesn't mean everyone was happy with integration." For the next thirty minutes, he went on to ask about my family's thoughts about moving south, my teaching assignment, salary, and other job-related questions. Then, the interview was over. He walked around his desk and shook my hand (I gave him a really good squeeze) and said, "Welcome aboard, young man!"

Dr. Floyd was waiting for me in the outer office. When we got in the car, he asked how the interview went. I said, "I honestly don't know; but I guess OK because I got the job!"

I learned later that Dr. Bryant had told Dr. Floyd, "I like that ole boy!"

When I got home, my fiancée asked the normal questions about shopping, housing, entertainment, and so on in Fort Pierce. I tried to be upbeat, but she sensed that the picture was not as rosy as I had painted it. However, she didn't press the issue.

On July 2, 1966, we got married. There was no honeymoon. On July 20, 1966, we left Akron. We arrived in Fort Pierce that evening, checked in to the only motel we saw on South Dixie Highway, and looked for a place to eat.

Every restaurant was closed, so I bought some chips and soft drinks from a 7-Eleven. The next morning, I planned to call Dr. Floyd after breakfast to tell him we were in town. That plan went to hell.

Ahead of us, as we drove down South Dixie Highway, I saw a sign that said, "South Dixie Restaurant." I told Pat to wait in the car until I could find out whether they were still serving breakfast. The first thing I noticed was that there were no Negroes in the restaurant. Everyone stopped eating to look at me.

They stared at me, in unison, as I approached the counter. I saw a poster of Dr. Martin Luther King Jr. in plain view. As I moved closer to the counter, I saw the caption under the picture, "Martin Luther Coon." Angrily, I turned, faced the customers and walked out the door. I didn't say a word to Pat about what I had experienced.

On the way out of the restaurant parking lot, there was a line of cars waiting to pick up their takeout orders. All of the drivers in the cars were Negroes. I drove until I saw a phone booth and called Dr. Floyd. He invited us to the junior college to have breakfast.

I never told Pat why we left the South Dixie Restaurant in such a hurry.

Dr. Floyd explained that the South Dixie was not off limits to Negroes, but most Negroes quit taking their business there because of the racist attitudes of the staff. Since the kitchen was out of sight to customers, Negroes never trusted what might be done to their food. I made a mental note to visit the restaurant again in the future. Pat was visibly upset. She would later refer to the city as "Fort Misery."

We found an apartment later that day and our furniture arrived two days later. Football practice was set to begin during the first week of August, so my wife and I explored Fort Pierce and later went to Miami Beach for an abbreviated honeymoon.

Football practice began two weeks before the start of school. In Florida, unlike Ohio, high schools were permitted to have spring practice. Coach Viland had been there in the spring and told me that the talent level was not as good as at Kenmore, but the players were hard workers. It was my understanding that Dan McCarty at one time had a great program and that we were brought in to raise it back to a place of prominence. From what I saw early on, it was going to take some time.

When school started, I learned that Dan McCarty had been integrated the year before. There were only a handful of Negro students and only one other Negro teacher—a math instructor transferred from Lincoln Park Academy, the Negro school. My teaching assignment was physical education in the mornings and English in the afternoons.

On my first day, I was on my way to the teachers' lounge when I noticed a female teacher standing outside her classroom as she ushered students to class—until she saw me. She quickly stepped back into her classroom. When I got well past her classroom, I glanced back. She was back on the walkway greeting students.

I continued to the teachers' lounge, which had separate areas for men and women. The only teachers I had met and talked with until then were the football coaches. When I walked into the men's lounge, I waved my hand and said hello to everyone. Except for Rudy Bretherick, the guys in the lounge politely spoke back. Rudy taught at Dan McCarty but was also the defensive coach at John Carroll, the Catholic high school. (In 1967 he became the head coach.) He had a booming voice and blurted out, "Hey, boy—high ya dooin!"

Did he just call me "boy?" My first instinct was to tell him that a 6'1", 200-pound "niggah" was not a "boy." I suppressed my street language and said, "Just fine, thanks." A few minutes later, another teacher entered the room and Rudy addressed him with the same greeting. It was just his way.

Rudy and I became pretty good friends as time passed. Then, one day several weeks later, we were talking and he told me that some of the teachers in the lounge told him after I had left that he might have offended me. He said, "I want to apologize if I did." I lied to ease his mind. I told him I was not offended, but black men do not appreciate being called "boy."

On Friday morning before our first football game, the cheerleaders organized a big pep rally. The band director, Harold Supank, the band, and the students were fired up. As rallies go, it was a good one until the band started playing "Dixie."

Everyone got up and started singing, "Oh, I wish I was in the land of cotton." Our team and coaches were sitting in the front of the gymnasium. To the right of us in the bleachers, two young men stood and started waving a huge Confederate flag, swiping the heads of four or five black students sitting in front of them. The black youngsters turn and ask them to stop, but they kept waving the flag, taunting the black students. The band stopped and they all sat down.

That evening, we lost the game. On the way back from the stadium, I asked Coach Viland whether he had seen what happened at the pep rally.

He told me he had and that it bothered him. I told him we needed to do something about it before it caused an altercation. He wanted to know whether I had any ideas.

I came up with a plan. When the coach approached the team with my idea, they thought it would be a great way to show their dislike for some of their classmates disrespecting colored students and their colored teammates.

On Friday morning at our second pep rally, the whole football team— black and white—was ready. When Supank's band began playing "Dixie," the whole team stood and waved the tiny Confederate flags we had purchased for them, using a sit-down motion toward the boys with the large Confederate flag.

Evidently, our plan had leaked. Several students sitting behind the team also had flags. Students were also sitting on both sides of the guys with the big flag waving their flags and shouting, "Sit down, Sit down."

Everyone looked toward the back of the gym. Mr. Lawrence Terry, the principal almost ran toward the two boys with the big flag. You could hear a pin drop. He motioned for the boys to come down from the bleachers. When they reached the floor, he marched them out of the gymnasium to a resounding cheer from most of the student body. The big flag was never seen again at pep rallies.

The team began the season 2–2, with the toughest part of the season still to begin. About then I noticed some changes among the women teachers. They started greeting me when I passed them. Some even sat down beside me in the cafeteria. I guess that the male teachers' attitude toward me had given them "permission" to speak to the colored guy. Progress was being made.

After our coaching staff had finished work one evening, someone suggested that we get something to eat. This was my opportunity. I said, "Let's go to the South Dixie. I hear they serve good Southern food." An awkward moment of silence followed, but then Chris Shay, our line coach, said he thought it was a great idea. Chris was a town guy who was well respected by everyone on and off campus. He played football at the University of South Carolina and had coached with "Hunk" Slay, the athletic director at Dan McCarty. Before becoming athletic director, Slay was McCarty's head football coach when the school had good football teams.

Fort Pierce is a small town. Everybody followed the football team and knew the coaches, including me. When we walked in, I was deliberately the last to enter. When they saw me, there were some cautious looks.

Chris said, loud enough for all to hear, "Ya'll know Coach Greene, don't you?" Chris's introduction forced them to acknowledge me. We sat and ordered. I was suspicious of what might happen in the kitchen, so I only ordered pie and coffee because I could see the pie in the case. Several people left the restaurant. A few stopped by our table on their way out and welcomed me to town. Several of those who stopped had young men on the football team. I never entered the establishment again during my time in Fort Pierce. Still, I had made a big first step.

The football team ended the season with a 4–6 record. Even though that was better than the previous year, it was still disappointing. But the turnaround excited the fans.

Between the end of the football season and the start of the Christmas season, Pat and I attended several parties in both the white and Negro communities. The Negro functions we attended were like Negro functions everywhere—good fun, dancing, real food, and lively discussions.

The white parties were a little more subdued. In those days, most whites in the South had been in few social settings with Negroes and they were feeling their way. Pat and I had much more experience in mixed-race social events, which made them comfortable with their decision to invite us. We always asked whether they had any dancing music, so we would get the party started.

I told my wife that we ought to try what comedian Dick Gregory had suggested in one of his routines—to start eating his mashed potatoes and chicken with our fingers just to see how the rest of the guests would react. Although we did not do that, it would have been interesting to see the reactions.

In the spring, I was asked to coach the track team. That meant an extra $500, so I accepted the job. We had a decent track team with three exceptional athletes. David Bishop was a state-ranked high jumper; Robin Blanton was state-ranked in the pole vault; and Ronnie Foss was state-ranked in the hurdles. All three were white kids who had earned track scholarships. Robin went on to the University of Florida and set school records. He now is an attorney in Gainesville, Florida. The other two went into the military.

We traveled all over Florida. During those trips, I learned a lot about the social structure in Fort Pierce and the attitudes regarding integration. The track program did not have any money, so I went to businesses in the community to ask for support. I got it. The only problem was I did not ask for or get clearance from "Hunk" Slay, the athletic director. When he found that I had been raising funds, "Hunk" called me into his office and chewed me out. It was my first reprimand, and I left his office thinking I had made an enemy.

I made many friends, white and Negro, in Fort Pierce, but all was not rosy. Pat got a job at the Indian River Junior College and was doing very well. Indian River was built because of integration. The black college had closed and merged with the white college.

During my wife's second year there, we got pregnant. Several months into the pregnancy, she applied for a leave of absence. During her time there, several white employees had requested and were given maternity leaves. Pat's request was denied.

My wife is not one to let things slide. Her position at the college allowed her access to records and what she found was jaw-dropping. Negro employees were being paid less than their white counterparts in similar positions. Negro professors were also being paid less than white professors.

Interestingly, the Negro employees knew what was going on but were afraid to speak up. To top it off, an administrator's girlfriend was given my wife's position as soon as Pat took unauthorized leave. With all of the facts in hand, she filed a complaint with the Department of Justice. When she told some of the Negro employees what she was going to do, they advised her not to do it.

She had already started the process and was not about to change her mind. Several weeks later, representatives from the Justice Department came to the college to review its practices. Several weeks after that, the decision came down. She had won her case. She was given a job equal to the one she had, plus back pay. The other Negroes on campus also benefited from her actions. Salaries were equalized, and black athletes received the same scholarships and jobs on campus as the white athletes. Negro faculty members feared retaliation, but they were assured that the Department of Justice would be monitoring the situation. I knew the decision did not sit too well with many in the white community, but Pat won because she proved she had been a victim of discrimination.

More good than bad happened to us in Fort Pierce. For one thing, I improved my public speaking. Although I had majored in speech and tele-communications in college, most of my public speaking opportunities had been in front of classmates.

I was asked to speak to many organizations in Fort Pierce such as Kiwanis Clubs, Lions Clubs, and so forth. I guess, as the first black coach at Dan McCarty, the city people wanted to get a close look at me. My speaking tour gave me the opportunity to meet many influential individuals in the white business community. They got to check me out, and I gained experience in public speaking that would serve me well throughout the rest of my coaching career.

At one of my speaking engagements, I met a gentleman who owned a department store and several other businesses. His son was a member of my track team. Shortly after I had given a luncheon speech at his Kiwanis Club, the business owner invited me to lunch later.

Two days later, at lunch, he told me his son thought a lot of me and that I was a fair man and a good teacher. I had never experienced any problems with any of the players, but I often wondered what they thought about me. I coached them like I had coached players in Ohio and, at times, I expressed my dissatisfaction with them in no uncertain terms during practice. Evidently, they had taken my moments of displeasure in a positive way. My conversation with that athlete's father gave me hope that the youth of this country were the ones who could solve the problem of the racial divide.

I learned later that father and son were big University of Florida football fans. They invited me to attend a couple of games with them so I could watch the Gators and Steve Spurrier, who became a Heisman Trophy winner, NFL quarterback, punter, and legendary college football head coach.

I had many similar interactions. One McCarty teacher, Jim Lundy, was rumored to have made the comment that he would not work with a "nigger." Jim and I got along very well and I never sensed any dislike during the times we interacted on campus. Actually, we had many common interests, including fishing. One morning in the teacher's lounge, he asked whether I would like to go fishing with him. We arranged to meet at his home early Saturday morning. When I got there, he invited me in. His wife, Sandy, still in her bathrobe, made breakfast for us.

It was an interesting dynamic: sitting at a kitchen table, having breakfast with a man who was rumored to have ill feelings toward Negroes with his wife still in her bathrobe. We all ate breakfast and Jim and I went fishing. There I took the opportunity to ask him about the rumor about him. He admitted that he had said that, but told me things had changed for him.

He said his family had ingrained racial prejudice in him and that I was the first Negro he ever had the opportunity to know personally. We continued fishing and talking, and the subject was never brought up again. In the fall of 1967, our second season at Dan McCarty went 2–8.

From my first coaching experience at The University of Akron, my goal was to become a full-time college football coach and then to become the head coach of the Cleveland Browns. So, after the season I began to pursue that dream. During the spring of 1967, I wrote an article on "Run and Shoot football" and sent it in to *Scholastic Coach Magazine*. To my surprise, they published the article and sent me a fifty-dollar check.

In the article, I wrote about how we practiced, called plays, and some basic things we were doing on offense. I began receiving mail from high school coaches from around the country wanting to discuss the Run and Shoot offense. Evidently the passing game, especially the way we ran it, was something different. I responded to every piece of mail I received.

One of the letters was from a high school coach in Arizona. He and I communicated over a period of months. In one letter, he suggested that I attend the American Football Coaches Association meeting because it would be a great opportunity to meet the top coaches in the country. Even though the convention was in New York City and money was scarce, I decided to go.

I did not know anyone at the convention, but I walked around and introduced myself to coaches—many of whom I had read about and seen on television. They were cordial but not friendly. I met and spoke to several coaches from Negro colleges, but it seemed I was the only Negro who approached and introduced himself to white coaches.

Coaches always fill the lobby at these conventions and small satellite bars are set up in strategic places. The lobby and those bars are filled day and night. They are the ultimate watering holes and most of the coaches are on expense accounts, so the liquor and beer flowed freely.

It struck me one evening while walking around the lobby that these satellite bars were segregated—not by design but still segregated. I saw little, if any, interaction between Negro coaches and white coaches. Then, I realized that I did not see any black coaches whose convention badges indicated they were on major college staffs. All the major colleges, with the exception of those in the deep south, had many Negro athletes but no Negro staff members.

Later that evening, I decided to go see some of New York. I headed down Broadway and stopped at a night club to have a beer. The place was loaded with coaches. After a few drinks, I sat down at the piano bar and began playing. Several coaches came up and asked who I was and where I coached. After a while, I got up to leave and I heard a voice yell: "Hey! Florida Ray? Come over here."

I went to the table and sat down with the coaching staff from the University of Connecticut. After exchanging pleasantries, the head coach, who had been drinking for a while, gave me a challenge. He scribbled his name—Tony Gerosciotti—on a napkin and told me that if I pronounced his name correctly, he would buy a round for the table. I knew right away how to pronounce it. Little did he did know I had grown up around Italians and, specifically, one family with that same name.

I said, "How about two rounds?"

"Sure, make it two rounds!" he said. He handed me the napkin.

I slowly began drawing out his first name, "Ton—y." Then, I spat out the last name in a burst: "jer-o-shoti!"

The assistant coaches chanted, "Florida Ray! Florida Ray! Florida Ray! Waitress! Waitress! Waitress!"

That night, I learned an important thing about the coaching and any other business, especially if you want to advance: it is not about who you know, but who knows you. By the end of that evening, my piano lessons paid off and several coaches knew my name and where I was from.

When the group got up to leave, Coach Gerosciotti gave me his card and told me to call him. It was a good night and a worthwhile trip. On Thursday evening, there was a huge banquet sponsored by Kodak. All of the conference champions of college football were honored. It was an impressive affair. I thought to myself that I was going to be on that dais at that convention in the future.

The following Monday morning, when I checked in at the school office, there was a pile of mail in my box from some of the universities I had written to several weeks previously.

While devising a plan to be a collegiate football coach, I had written letters applying for collegiate assistant coaching positions. I didn't have a clue how to get into college coaching. So, my plan began by buying a copy of *Street and Smith's Annual Football Preview* magazine and having some personal stationery printed.

I am not a good typist, but I typed letters to 120 colleges, applying for a coaching job, and mailed them. I received eighty replies. Most of the replies were similar: "Thank you for your letter. At the present time we have no openings on our staff. However, we will keep your resume on file and if something changes, we will contact you."

After a while, I went through the letters again. Among the form letters thirty-one of them, I surmised, were dictated to a secretary from the head coach. I typed a second letter to them where I thanked them for their encouragement and assured them that they would get a good football coach if they hired me.

I asked for an in-person interview if and when they had a position open. A few weeks later, the replies began to come in. Many of the letters said basically the same thing as the first batch of replies. Nine of the letters asked me whether I would be interested in a graduate assistant's position. If so, I should send them my information. I sent information to all of them. I received several offers outlining what the grad assistant job entailed. However, I could not afford to take any of the positions. The salary range for all of them was between $1,200 and $1,600 a semester, with no free graduate school. With a newborn and wife to support, I was back at square one.

A BETTER OFFER

One of the letters in that pile was from the University of Miami. I had forgotten I had applied there regarding a pilot program it was starting. When public schools were desegregated, none of the Negro administrators at black schools got administrative positions at the newly integrated schools. When the Negro schools closed, the administrators were relegated to positions as teachers, or went to work in a federally funded program in the schools.

They did not become administrators, it was intimated, because they had no experience working with white parents or students. Though it was true, it was also true that the white administrators had no experience working with Negro students or parents. There was no logic here, but that was the way it was.

Miami's pilot program was designed to train administrators to work in multicultural situations. I started to develop another plan. I would apply for one of the scholarships and, if I got it, I would ask the football coach whether I could volunteer to be a graduate assistant at Miami.

The scholarship paid more money, and Miami was only two hours from Fort Pierce, which meant I would not have to move. I knew that several administrators and teachers in Fort Pierce, who were displaced because of integration, were also applying. Among them were principals, teachers with master's degrees, and several Negro businessmen, and that was only in Fort Pierce.

I did not think I had much chance of being selected for the program, but I was shocked to find that there were three hundred applicants being considered for twenty-six positions. I called Coach Gerosciotti, who said that that I had impressed him last week. He knew I wanted to get into college coaching, so he thought he would make me an offer. I was at a loss for words for a moment, but I managed to ask what the offer was. He needed a graduate assistant. I could help coach, stay in student housing, go to grad school free, and receive a stipend of $2,200. Before I could say anything, he asked whether I was married. He suggested I talk it over with Pat before making a decision.

That evening, Pat and I discussed the offer. We would have to move to Connecticut. The salary was only $2,200 for the year and we would have to live meagerly. She was not a fan of "Fort Misery," although she did like the beaches, so moving was not out of the question. She also felt we could make it financially for a year, since we could live on campus in married student housing. She told me it was up to me.

I thought about it overnight. The next morning, I told her I would take the offer, but first, I wanted to explore more of the possibilities in a few of the letters. I called Tony and told him we were considering his offer, and I asked when he needed a decision. He said everything would be fine if I got there by the middle of August.

Two days later, a letter with the University of Miami logo arrived at my door. To my surprise, when I opened the letter, the first thing I saw was, "Congratulations!" I had been accepted into the Multicultural Scholarship Program.

All participants were to report to Miami on August 15 for orientation. To say the least, I was shocked and pleasantly surprised at the same time. Pat was more excited than me and she told me to go to Miami. I told her that the scholarship had nothing to do with football, and I wanted to coach. She told me to think about it and make a decision.

On the morning of August 15, 1968, I got up early, got dressed, ate breakfast, and headed south to Miami. By 9:15, I was sitting in the football office waiting to see Charlie Tate, the head football coach. I told his secretary it was about a private matter. About a half hour later, her phone rang and she told me Coach Tate would see me. I did not hear the secretary tell him I was a Negro, but he exhibited no surprise when I walked in. He gave me a friendly greeting, shook my hand, and told me to have a seat. Coach Tate had a cherub-looking face and steel-gray hair. He is the type of person that people instantly like.

He asked me, "What brings you to Miami?"

I only had this one chance to impress him. I said, "Coach Tate, I want to coach college football." I mentioned that I had read his book on the "Four Spoke Defense" and that I felt I could learn a lot about the game from him. I continued, "Later this morning, I have an orientation for a scholarship I received from the university. I have also been offered a graduate assistantship at the University of Connecticut. This is the first of two stops I am going to make on campus today. If you'll give me the opportunity to work as a graduate assistant on your staff, I'll do it for free. If you can't, at eleven o'clock I am going over to the Graduate School and tell them I can't accept the scholarship and I am going to Connecticut." I got it all out in one breath.

He studied me for a moment before he spoke. "I like your enthusiasm!" We talked for about twenty-five minutes more. He wanted to know about my background, my family, and he questioned me about football. I did not know a lot, but I knew about the Run and Shoot, and that interested him. He told me he wanted to talk to me about that offense and some of the duties I would have after I had gotten settled.

"Does that mean that I am hired?" I asked.

He said, "Yes, but I can't pay you."

I told him I understood. (I probably shouldn't have told him that, but it was the truth.)

It was nearly ten thirty, so I left his office mission accomplished and headed to the graduate school. On the way over, I thought about how I would tell Tony that I was not coming to Connecticut.

After the orientation, I called Tony collect from campus. He told me that he understood and left me with some sound advice: coaching is a fluid business and family should always be the first consideration. In less than four hours, everything I wanted had come to fruition.

When the news that I was going to Miami reached Fort Pierce, there were a lot of congratulations and the coaches at Dan McCarty gave me a farewell party.

In 1968, I left Fort Pierce to go to Miami. I wasn't sure whether it was because of the Civil Rights Movement, the continued desegregation of Fort Pierce, or the assassinations of Martin Luther King Jr. and Bobby Kennedy. I just knew I wanted to leave.

POSTSCRIPT / FORT PIERCE

I experienced several racial problems in Fort Pierce. For example, in some stores, when receiving change from a purchase, some of the women cashiers would drop the money into my hand, rather than risk touching me. I would linger to watch whether they did the same with white customers. They didn't. Some would say it is a "little" thing, but we live with our antennas up. I chalked it up to ignorance. These, and several other instances, were minor, but I took some gratification in seeing Fort Pierce adapting to change.

The most serious issue, however, was a letter that told me if I stepped on the field, I would be shot. It caused me concern and the police kept a watchful eye during games. Strangely, I do not remember being afraid. Other than that, in a couple of places we played, the opponent's fans made some derisive remarks. Once, in typical fashion, our receivers and quarterbacks took the field about forty-five minutes before the game in Melbourne, Florida. As I walked across the field toward the Melbourne sideline, I heard a fan shout, "Hey Spanky, what you doin' out there—you lost? When they start letting niggahs coach? You forgot your spear—you lost?"

I just smiled and waved to the man speaking. Although the schools were integrated, segregation still existed inside the schools. Black students who now attended previously all-white schools usually were not invited to participate in school clubs and activities and were strategically placed in classes together. The real integration occurred on athletic teams, where white coaches were happy to have some of the talented black youngsters who now attended their schools.

In Fort Pierce, black high schools still existed. Lincoln Park Academy, the black high school, competed against other black schools but did not play against the newly integrated schools. We never played against Lincoln Park, even though we were in the same city, less than ten minutes apart.

The integration of schools was not smooth. There was still the notion that black athletes were not coachable. As an example, I remember the Boy's State Basketball Tournament of March 1968. Previously there had been two tournaments—one colored and one white.

As the tournament progressed, it came down to Orlando Evans, an all-white team, and Key West. The Key West team had a white coach, but all of their players were black—the result of integration and the recent phasing out of another, all-black high school. Key West was derided in the buildup to the game: "They play street ball." "They can't handle Evans' Zone Press." "They are undisciplined, etc."

There was a full house at the University of Florida when the two teams took the floor. Anticipation was high. Key West took the lead before the half and never looked back. It was no contest after halftime. People were almost apologetic for the comments they had made about Key West. Reality set in. Florida basketball would never be the same.

MIAMI

Miami's football team reported two weeks before the start of school. Classes did not start until after Labor Day. I should have stayed home with my pregnant wife until I had to report to school. However, I felt I had to go to campus early to begin studying what the team was doing on offense and defense. So, on August 20, 1968, I headed to Miami. Luckily, I had some great neighbors who kept in close touch with my wife.

Coach Tate was surprised to see me, but when I explained to him why I had come early, he seemed impressed. I could never tell for sure what

Charlie was thinking. All of the coaches were busy in their offices when he took me around to introduce me. They were cordial, but busy, and eager to get back to work. Coach took me to the equipment man, who provided me with a locker and coaching clothes. After finishing outfitting me, Coach Tate took me back to his office.

Coach Tate told me that I would basically be a gofer. I must have had a strange look on my face because he explained that a *gofer* works at his and the assistant coaches' pleasure and "goes for this and he goes for that." I told him I had been a gofer before and understood what it entailed. However, this time, if I was going to be an errand boy, I made up my mind I would be much more than a gofer.

The married student's dorm would not be available for two weeks, so I slept in my van. I got up at six a.m. and studied the playbook until about seven-thirty. Then, I went to the football office, took a shower, and went to the film room. When the coaches came in, they saw me watching.

They always said hello and went about their business until they needed the room. I then went to one of their offices to continue studying. From time to time, they called me and asked me to do something for them. I got to know the secretary pretty well, because she was there every morning when I came in. Three or four days later, she asked me where I was living. My first inclination was to lie and tell her I was staying at a motel. However, I sensed she knew better, so I told her the truth and asked her not to tell Coach Tate. I don't know for sure, but I believe she did tell him.

During the two weeks before classes, I spent eight to ten hours a day in the football office. The only time I was not working on football was when I ate or had to run an errand for one of the coaches.

The player I talked to the most was Ted "the Mad Stork" Hendricks. Ted was an All-American who went on to become a great All-Pro linebacker in the NFL with the Baltimore Colts and Oakland Raiders. He was 6'7" tall. That didn't surprise me, but I was shocked that he only weighed 218 pounds. His nickname suited him. It was hard to believe he would be strong enough to be a great pro player, but he was.

Ted, an upcoming senior, was fun-loving and we got along well. I am sure he told the other players about me because when I went to the first practice, several of them greeted me as Coach Greene. My relationship with Ted had gotten me respect. Now, I had to earn it.

Coach Tate assigned me to work with Walt Kichefski. Walt was the linebacker coach and the players loved and respected him. I was fortunate to help coach perhaps the two best outside linebackers in the nation, Ted Hendricks and Tony Cline. Both would play nine or ten years in the NFL for the Colts and the Raiders. Ted played five years with the Colts before going to the Raiders in 1975. Tony, who was a year behind Ted, played with the Raiders through the 1975 season, so he and Ted were both playing for the Raiders together for a season.

Tony spent the next two seasons with the San Francisco 49ers. I don't know, to this day, whether two outside linebackers from the same school have ever started for the same team in the NFL, but I had the opportunity to coach both of them.

The opportunity came sooner than I had expected. After calisthenics, we went into "individual"—when the position coaches run drills with their players. Walt yelled out to me, "Ray, you take the left side and I'll take the right." Ted played on the left side. I knew immediately that Walt would ask Ted's opinion about how I ran the drills. Evidently, I did OK, because Walt involved me in his meetings and on the field.

When classes started, I spent every moment when I was not in class or studying in the football office. Coach Tate did not talk to me very much but stopped by the film room sometimes to ask how school was going or just to say hello. He had to have known what was going on. He was on top of everything.

I learned a lot from Charlie Tate. I have never met another coach, to this day, who was more knowledgeable about football—he was like a walking encyclopedia. Coach Tate created the "Four Spoke Defense" while he was an assistant at Georgia Tech. It is now referred to as "Two-Deep Coverage." He was fluent in all phases of football and it amazed me in staff meetings that he could always give in-depth solutions to any situation on offense, defense, or the kicking game.

Other than his vast knowledge of the game, he had a unique personality and approach to players. During practice, he always wore a baseball cap and sunglasses, and he continually chewed on a cigar. He was not a tall man, but he had a booming voice. He ran a spirited practice and, at times, he would get all over a player who had made a mistake. He reminded me of a father disciplining his child and the players seemed to take it that way. They were eager to please him.

If Coach Tate chewed out a player, sometime during or after practice I would hear him praising the player for something he did right. Few left the practice field upset at being reprimanded. That could not have been a better learning experience for me as a young coach.

That season during *two-a-days*—two full practices every day—I went home on weekends. When I couldn't, Pat would drive to Miami. Once the season started, it was an exciting time for me. The University of Miami is a different kind of place. Walking around campus during game week, there were no banners or student activities like the ones at Ohio State or Akron. It was warm and the pool in the middle of campus was always busy. Generally, the students did not show much interest in the upcoming football game.

Surprisingly, when we showed up at the Orange Bowl, there were about 40,000 people there. The native Miamians evidently wanted to see Ted Hendricks and other local stars. Our first game was with Northwestern. They had huge offensive and defensive lines, typical of Big Ten teams, but they were no match for our speed. The final score was 28–7, Miami Hurricanes.

I had not told my classmates in the graduate program that I was on the football staff and when I showed up at a party after the game, they treated me as though I had scored the touchdowns. Our class was evenly divided— fourteen Negroes and twelve whites. (I thought there would be more Negroes, since they were the ones who had been displaced.) They clapped, and told me, "you have just made history."

As far as I know, I was the first black coach to walk the sideline in a Division I football program in the South and maybe the nation. I did not bother to tell them that I was a graduate assistant, but I don't think it would have mattered to them.

We had two Negro athletes on the team, Tom Sullivan and Ray Bellamy. Both were outstanding athletes. Tom was a running back and Ray a wide receiver. Tom went on to play with the Philadelphia Eagles for several years. Ray had a chance to be a great pro, but an automobile accident curtailed that opportunity. He is now doing great things at Florida A&M University. They also made history. Ray was the first scholarship athlete signed at Miami; Tom signed later the same recruiting year. Watching Miami now, it is hard to imagine only two black athletes on a Miami team.

The Hurricanes won five of the first seven games. We beat Georgia Tech 10–7, LSU 30–0, Virginia Tech 13–8, and Pitt 48–0. We lost to USC 28–3 and Auburn 31–6. Ray Bellamy played great for us. In many games, he was the only black player on the field. In the sixth game, in late October against Auburn, which had no black athletes, it appeared he was on the defense's hit list. Auburn's pass rush overwhelmed and shut down our offense. They also hit Bellamy late, double-covered him, and interfered on a certain touchdown catch. Nothing was called. I heard that "Shug" Jordan, the Auburn coach, on his Sunday show said a key to victory was "corralling" that colored boy Bellamy. I had never met the man, but I instantly disliked him.

Unfortunately, the last half of our season was a disaster. We beat Pittsburgh after the Auburn loss and went on to lose the last three games of the season to Penn State, Alabama, and Florida.

We were a better team than our 5–5 record indicated. I got into the habit of asking why we didn't do better after our first loss of the season to USC. I found we did not play the kicking game very well and that we needed to be in better physical condition—especially our big guys. Late in the season, during our losing streak, the school paper severely criticized the team and coaches, and I saw the negative effect it had on our team. Student involvement and support is absolutely necessary to have a winning program.

Throughout the football season in 1968, there were almost daily reports in the newspaper about black athletes in the North protesting the manner in which they were being treated. These protests followed the ones that occurred during the October 1968 Olympics in Mexico City. During the medal ceremony on October 16, two black athletes, Tommie Smith and John Carlos, took a stand for civil rights by raising their black-gloved fists and wearing human rights badges and black socks in lieu of shoes.

As punishment, the International Olympic Committee banned Smith and Carlos from the Olympics for life. They had won gold and bronze medals, respectively, in the 200-meter race. Their protest stirred controversy worldwide, especially in the United States. Most Negroes applauded their sacrifice because it ignited a conversation about the treatment of blacks in America.

The Silver Medalist in that event, Peter Norman of Australia, also wore an Olympic Project for Human Rights badge on the podium in support of his fellow competitors. Norman's action was not widely reported, but the Australian Olympic team left Norman off the roster for the 1972 Games.

These were not the first black athletes to protest the treatment of black athletes in America. In 1960, Cassius Clay of Louisville, Kentucky, won Olympic gold as a heavyweight boxer. It was reported that, in a show of disgust, Clay threw his gold medal into the Ohio River to make a political statement.

Though he was highly criticized, Clay became heavyweight champion of the world as a pro. Shortly after winning that title, he became a Muslim and changed his name to Muhammed Ali. Because of his religious beliefs, he refused to serve in the Army during the Vietnam War. As a result, he was stripped of his title. In Fort Pierce at the time, there was much hatred for Ali and I was often asked my opinion about the matter. Although there were two Negroes working at Dan McCarty, I was the only one involved in athletics. I never got into any long conversations about it other than to state my disagreement with the decision.

Black athlete protests were gaining momentum. Those protests opened the door for me to get into college coaching as a full-time assistant coach.

In the spring of 1969, Coach Tate called me to his office. Eddie Crowder, the head coach at the University of Colorado, called and told him he wanted to hire a black coach (by this time, as I remember it, Negroes had become "black"). Word had spread that Miami had a black coach—me. Coach told me that Crowder wanted to interview me for the position if I was interested. Naturally, I was interested, but first I wanted to know if Coach Tate anticipated any openings on the Miami staff. He didn't, and he told me I should go for the interview. He cautioned me to not accept any position that was not an "on-the-field job," or that had not been held by a white coach.

When I asked why he said, "Ray, things are changing, but if you are not offered a job under the conditions I just told you, it could turn out bad." I was curious why he would dissuade me from taking a job at a Big Eight school—the most dominant conference in the country at the time.

"If he tells you that he wants you to be the mentor to his black athletes or handle their problems, what happens if they continue to protest or they don't trust you because you are not a position coach? I will tell you what will happen! You will get fired and he will hire another black coach who he thinks can 'handle' the black athletes." What Coach Tate said made sense.

I told him I understood. His last bit of advice to me was to call Coach Crowder before taking the trip and ask him about the position. I told him I would. That evening, I called.

After a friendly preliminary conversation, I asked Coach Crowder what position I would be coaching. He paused and admitted he did not have a position open—basically he was creating a position where I would work as a liaison between the black athletes and the coaching staff. Coach Tate had been prophetic. I tried to not show my disappointment, thanked him, and told him I looked forward to meeting him. The next day, I called his office and informed them I was not coming.

In 1968, teams in the South saw little integration of players. In the North, integrated teams were not unusual. However, to the best of my recollection, the only black coach at a major university at that time was Frank Gilliam at the University of Iowa. He had been hired before black athletes began exerting their demands in the Big Eight, Pac 10, Big Ten and other major northern conferences. Black athletes protesting was the catalyst that initiated major universities to seriously consider hiring black coaches. However, long before the protests in the 1960s, black athletes who wanted to play major college football in the North or South encountered much resentment.

Around midnight, two weeks after the Colorado job offer, I was studying when I heard a loud knock on my apartment door. Opening the door, I saw LeRoy Pearce, Miami's offensive coordinator.

He appeared to be a bit anxious. He asked me, "Do you want a job?"

I eagerly said yes. LeRoy had been coaching more than twenty years. At the University of Tennessee, he coached Johnny Majors. Majors was an All-American and runner-up to Paul Hornung for the Heisman Trophy. He was now the head coach at Iowa State University.

LeRoy told me he had just spoken with Majors. When he learned that Majors was looking to hire a black coach, LeRoy thought of me. I doubt that LeRoy knew any other black coaches and the two of us had never really talked much during my time at Miami. I guess sometimes luck, or fate, plays an important role in success. I was in the right place at the right time. I learned something else from that experience: you never know who is watching, so it is a good idea to be your best self at all times. Although I had not had much contact with LeRoy, he evidently had observed me enough to put his word on the line and recommend me.

I thought to myself: here we go again. But as we discussed the job, LeRoy told me Jackie Sherrill had moved up from scout team coach to line-backer coach and Majors need to replace his position. It was sounding better. The job that was open was not a new job: it was Sherril's old job. I told LeRoy I was definitely interested. LeRoy contacted Coach Majors the next day, and a ticket was wired to me to make the trip to Iowa. However, first, I had to get permission to leave from Dr. Gordon Foster, the Dean of the Graduate School and director of my graduate studies program. Dr. Foster gave me the rest of the week off. On Thursday afternoon, I left for Ames, Iowa.

My graduate program at Miami was the first of its kind. It was designed specifically to train administrators to work in multicultural schools. We took the normal required classes in administration and supervision, but we experimented with many hands-on activities designed to prepare us once we became school administrators.

My primary reason for going to graduate school was that I thought I needed a master's degree to coach college football. It was a step toward achieving my goal of being a head coach on the Division I or professional level. However, it soon became much more.

The people who were in my class were teachers, displaced school administrators, and a few businessmen. We participated in role-playing activities designed to take positions that would cause conflict. The primary purpose was to determine ways to resolve conflicts that might occur in multiracial situations. These activities would be of great benefit to me in my future career as a coach.

One of the most helpful activities we participated in was a three-day, three-night workshop on "sensitivity training." After a day and a half of amicable dialogue, fatigue set in and class members began revealing what they really thought about one another. For some, it was a pitiful sight observing how they reacted when they heard what some of their class-mates really thought about them.

For me, it was a revelation. I am not the sharpest tool in the shed. However, in most groups, if testing means anything, I was always among the top one-third. I know I can be a bit assertive and thought I might get raked over the coals in the sessions. However, when my time came, the comments about me were nearly all complimentary and positive. I am not sure why that was, but it has always been that way. I am good with groups. I make no conscious effort to lead, but somehow I always end up leading.

A couple of days after the sensitivity session, Dr. Foster told me that I was what those who study group dynamics call a *facilitator*—someone who enables others and helps the group reach a consensus. I did not know how I was doing it, but it seemed like a good thing to just continue being me.

When I left Miami International on Thursday afternoon, it was eighty degrees. When I arrived in Ames, Iowa, it was seventeen. A graduate assistant met me at the airport and checked me into the Holiday Inn. A short time later, Coach Majors called and told me to get some rest and that he would come by in the morning to take me to breakfast.

When I settled in, I turned on the television. Surfing through the channels, I found the Iowa State Girls Basketball Tournament. During the 1960s, women's basketball was not a popular sport. They did not play full court as they do now. The powers that be thought that young women were not physically able to do that. They played on the full court, but the teams were divided into offensive and defensive units on each side of the half-court line. Only those on the offensive end could score for each team. It was really a boring game.

Just as I started to resume surfing, the TV camera panned across the fans in the Des Moines arena. The announcer said the 14,000 people viewing the game was the largest crowd to view a girl's championship game. I was amazed that that many people would actually pay to watch girls play. Watching the game forced me to overcome my initial male chauvinist thoughts and realize that this was an exciting game. I later learned that Iowa was light years ahead of the rest of the country with regard to women's sports.

The next morning, at breakfast, Coach Majors asked me the usual questions about my family, where I grew up, where had I had coached, and so forth. Since all the answers were already on my resumé, I believe he just wanted to hear how I spoke and handled myself.

Although Majors grew up in Tennessee around black people, he had little experience dealing with educated black men or athletes. As strange as it may seem, I know of several times when a black person did not get a position because of his dialect, even though his use of the language was excellent. Right or wrong, I felt he harbored some of these stereotypical beliefs.

In any case, I am sure that if he was testing my ability to communicate, I passed that test. Since I would be representing him and the university, I understood. It still is a sad commentary considering I had a more extensive formal education than him.

Gordon Larson, my coach at South High and The University of Akron, often spoke to us about how to dress. One of his favorite statements was, "A college education ain't worth a nickel unless you feel comfortable in a suit and tie." It was good advice, then and now. I was dressed for the occasion.

After breakfast, Coach Majors gave me a tour of the campus and introduced me to several people, including some prominent alumni. Majors seemed a little tense. At the time I wondered if he had ever spent three hours alone with a black person. Later, I came to learn that that was just his way.

After the tour, we went to lunch at the Faculty Club. Majors had arranged for me to meet the university president, Dr. Robert Parks, athletic director Clay Stapleton, and several other administrators. None ate lunch with us. My thought was that they just wanted to check me out; I tried to dismiss this, but my antenna was up, and I wondered if the other assistants Majors hired went to the Faculty Club and were introduced to the president of the university. While we had lunch at the University Club, I noticed I was the only black person in the place, including the waiters. I later learned there were several black faculty members at ISU who ate there regularly.

While on this subject, I must say something about Iowa and its people. Iowa's black population is only a small percentage of its people. Most live in either Des Moines, Davenport, or East Waterloo. Iowa is a farming state, and hard work is not foreign to them. I genuinely believe that most Iowans are Americans who are more concerned about character than color, and it is one of the most pleasant places I have lived, except for the weather. I grew up in Ohio and am familiar with cold weather, but Iowa cold is a different kind of cold.

After lunch, we went to the football office and met the coaching staff. I spent time with each of them—Gordon Smith, Jackie Sherrill, Jimmy Johnson, King Block, Ollie Keller, and George Haffner. At that time, Iowa State was at the bottom of the Big Eight Conference, along with Oklahoma State and Kansas State. They were in a big-time conference but did not match up with Oklahoma, Nebraska, Colorado, Missouri, and Kansas.

Coach Majors was hired to change the culture of losing, and I wanted to be a part of it. I spent most of the afternoon visiting with the coaches and watching film. Later that evening, we had dinner with his family at their home. His wife, Mary Lynn, was the perfect hostess. I don't know whether she had ever cooked for, or served dinner to, a black person, but she did a great job. Southern charm is something to be admired.

After dinner, John and I went into his den and the real discussion began. His first question was, "Who is this guy 'Hunk' Slay?" I immediately thought about how I solicited funds for the Dan McCarty track team in Fort Pierce without his permission and how he chewed me out for it.

My mind raced to figure out how I could overcome Hunk's bad evaluation of me. I told Coach Majors that Hunk was the athletic director at McCarty. To my surprise, Majors said he had never heard a more complimentary endorsement than Hunk had given me. Hunk told him about the fundraising I had done and said that I was a real "go-getter."

Coach Majors told me the salary was $15,500 and what my responsibilities would be. Even though this was a decent salary for 1969, it was a pay cut because I had been offered $19,000 to be an assistant principal in Miami. He also told me he wanted me to recruit in Georgia and Florida. I told him I knew of several big-time players in Miami and South Florida.

He expressed some doubt about being able to recruit Florida kids to Iowa. I told him I knew I could, but I could tell he didn't believe me. Finally, when he thought the time was right, he asked me, "What do you think about black athletes dating white girls?"

Many Southern white men have nightmares about this, but I never thought it would come up in an interview for a coaching job. I thought for a while and told him, "Coach, it isn't my business who they date but, considering the racial attitudes that exist, my advice to them would be to avoid it."

I then said, "Coach, let's say you attended Grambling University. Grambling is a predominately black university in a predominately black town, just the opposite of Ames, Iowa. Do you think you might date a black girl if you were at Grambling?" He looked at me and told me he understood my point.

The questioning went on. Majors said he liked clean-shaven athletes with neat haircuts instead of afros. I told him that times were changing and, as coaches, we have to change with the times. Making a big deal of it would only detract from our objective of building a winning program. When I used the words "our objective," my immediate thought reminded me of my discussion with Dr. Foster about being a facilitator. It was not calculated, but I had just given Coach Majors an opportunity to be a part of my thinking, and he had accepted my premise.

He had one more question: What about moustaches and beards? I told him that most black men have one or the other or both. He countered, "You don't have one!"

"Trust me, coach, I've tried but mine looked so raggedy, I decided to quit trying." He laughed and said we would not let hair be a factor. But, during the season, we want them trimmed and neat. He actually said "we." I knew then that I had the job.

I had been under the impression that a master's degree was required to coach in college, but Coach Majors told me it wasn't necessary. Regardless, I told him that I wanted to complete grad school.

Spring practice would begin in a month and I needed to be there. The question was, how could I do both—finish school in Miami and coach during spring practice in Ames?

Driving back to the hotel after dinner, Coach Majors spoke about his philosophy of coaching. He believed in discipline and thought that was the key to changing the culture at ISU. During our time together over two days, he never mentioned anything about problems at ISU or elsewhere regarding black athletes. However, I was soon made aware of a serious situation that had recently occurred on Iowa State's campus.

It was about eleven p.m. I had just hung up the phone relating the day's events to Pat, when my phone rang. Dan Robinson, a former ISU player who was now in grad school, called to tell me that the black athletes wanted to meet me.

I told him that I was leaving the next day. "They want to meet with you now!" I had some reservations. I was in a strange town, I did not know this person, and it was late. His voice sounded Midwestern, like mine. He could have been a member of the Klan, I thought. With some reluctance, I agreed to go with him to meet the athletes.

A few minutes later, Dan called my room and said he was in the lobby. When I went to meet him, I saw a big, young black man standing at the front desk. When he saw me, he came over, shook my hand and formally introduced himself. Dan, at 6'4", 275 pounds, had been an offensive tackle for ISU. He did not play his fourth year. He was an impressive-looking and well-spoken young man.

As we drove off, he told me several athletes were waiting for me at his apartment. When we entered his apartment, I saw seventeen or eighteen of ISU's black athletes, mostly football players, staring at me.

Dan introduced me and asked me to tell the players about myself. I did and then asked if they had any questions for me. "Did Coach Majors tell you anything about what is going on here?" one asked.

I briefly outlined some of the things I had discussed with Majors.

"Did he talk about our demands?" another asked.

I could only answer no. I could tell they were an organized group because the conversation had order. However, I sensed some anger.

Black college athletes were organizing all over the country in 1968, and this was also the case, I learned, in Ames. The previous spring, twenty-five Iowa State athletes had complained to the Iowa State Athletic Council of discriminatory treatment by some coaches. They made demands. They wanted the baseball and the basketball coach to change their attitudes toward black players or be fired. They wanted lineups in every sport to be based on ability and not on a black-white quota. They wanted to be called "Afro-Americans" or "blacks," not "Negroes." They wanted permission to hold jobs during the school year, because the families of black athletes were mostly low-income. They also demanded that Iowa State hire a black head coach or assistant and a black administrator in athletics. Perhaps because many student protesters were football players, and perhaps because they supported Coach Majors, they especially wanted a black football coach. At first, the ISU administration played off the complaints as the result of misunderstandings and defended their coaches as being free from prejudice. Over the summer the black students had to renew their demands. Twenty-four of the twenty-five threatened to withdraw from the school. In August the administration made some concessions but rebuffed their demand for a black football coach. The black athletes were told that it would violate Coach Majors' academic freedom and restrict his ability to recruit freely. The protesting athletes were not all satisfied. Two football players, star defensive lineman Willie Muldrew and Dan Graves, withdrew from the school.

First, I skimmed an article they provided. Then, I reread it more carefully. I thought, "What the hell have I gotten myself into?" The players, most of whom had attended the earlier meeting with the ISU Athletic Council, all had their eyes trained on me studying my reaction. I could feel the tension in the room. Before I spoke, I fought to control my anger about not being told about all this. I scanned the room, looking at each athlete directly in his eyes.

"Gentlemen, of course you understand that I don't know what you have been experiencing here at ISU. Based on what I have read about demands being made by black athletes on other campuses, I do understand and agree with them.

"Coach Majors has offered me a coaching position on his staff. However, before accepting the position, I am going to ask him to agree to a meeting with the Black Students Organization to discuss the complaints you have made. My objective in asking for this meeting, and subsequent meetings if necessary, will be to resolve the issues you presented to the Athletic Council that are affecting black students on campus and in the athletic department."

One of the athletes asked, "When are you going to ask him? What if he refuses to meet with us?"

I looked him dead in the eye. "I'll speak with him when I return for spring practice in a few weeks. If he refuses to meet with you, you'll be having another meeting like this one in a couple of weeks, with a new candidate for the coaching position."

A buzz went around the room. They would not forget what I had promised them. I remained for a short while before asking Dan to take me back to the hotel. It was two in the morning and my plane was departing at 6:50 a.m. It wouldn't matter. I wasn't going to sleep anyway. I had much to consider. I dozed a little but found myself smiling as I remembered what I had learned from one of the graduate classes I had taken at Miami—Conflict Resolution.

FROM HURRICANES TO CYCLONES

On the way back to Miami, I considered how to approach Dr. Foster about having to miss four weeks of classes to attend spring practice at Iowa State. His office was my first stop Monday morning.

He was aware of my trip and asked how it went. I told him it went well and that I had been offered a position. In discussing the four weeks of classes I would miss, I told him that I planned to finish the program and explained that I had done well in all of my classes. The only real task I had left was to complete term papers for my two classes. Dr. Foster thought for a moment before agreeing to let me complete the program as long as my professors allowed me to write the papers while in Iowa. I knew they would.

Coach Tate's office was my next stop. It was déjà vu all over again, as Yogi Berra would say. This time, however, was completely different from my first visit to his office more than a year ago.

Charlie got up from behind his desk and came across the room to shake my hand. (I knew then that Majors had already spoken with him.) "Congratulations! You must have been impressive because Johnny went on and on about you."

I knew Coach Tate had given me a good recommendation and I told him how much I appreciated his help. He said, "I recommended you because of the work you have done here. You were in the office looking at film every time I passed by the film room, you fit in well, and you always contributed more than you were asked to."

When he said that I fit in, it reminded me of the phrase he often used when coaching quarterbacks not to throw the ball into an area congested with defenders: "Don't force it where it doesn't fit." I used that phrase for the rest of my coaching career.

Next, I went back to my apartment to call Hunk Slay, who immediately asked if I had gotten the job. I told him I appreciated his recommendation and that I was a little surprised because I remembered how angry he was about me raising funds without permission.

"I was angry," he told me, "But not for the reason you thought. I was very impressed with the way you handled yourself here. Your attitude and your demeanor with students and faculty prevented many problems. You changed a lot of attitudes among people who had never known a black man on a personal or professional level. When I got upset with you, and I was not that upset, I considered it a learning experience for you.

"I wish you'd enlisted my assistance because I could have helped, but now I know you'll remember to follow procedure. I admired your initiative and I knew you were doing it for the athletes—not for yourself. That was important to me. That is important because I think you will go far in the coaching business."

When we hung up, I thought about the turmoil in America—the assassinations of the Kennedys and King; the dogs and church bombings in Birmingham; the march to Montgomery; the Edmund Pettus Bridge; Medgar Evers; Chaney, Goodman, and Schwerner; George Wallace in Alabama; Autherine Lucy; Emmett Till; the riots; and all that had happened as a result of the racial divide.

My conversation with Hunk gave me a glimpse of what the future might hold in penetrating the pervasiveness of racial attitudes. Hunk was a truly Southern white man, but he was decent, caring, and rose above color to assist a young black man. I thought there had to be many white people like Hunk who would adjust to changing times. It has been a slow process. Even today, many seek to reverse the progress made and to move America backwards.

SPRING PRACTICE

I sat in my first staff meeting as a full-time major college coach. I had met all of the coaches, except the freshman coach, Joe Avezzano, and Jim Dyar, a graduate assistant. Frank Randall, the trainer, was also there. Frank gave an update on the physical condition of the team and left.

The most time-consuming portion of the staff meeting was putting each player in his correct position on the personnel boards and depth charts. The boards were color-coded for offense and defense. The first team was red, second gold, third black, and fourth brown.

The guys on the brown list—who were often referred to as "turds" by Coach Majors—would probably never play. They were my scout team. Overall, talent was meager at best. The depth charts had no resemblance to those of Miami.

I considered myself the head coach of the scout team. Our job was to present a good picture of our opponents' plays against our first- and second-team defense. It was brutal for the brown squad, and they got beaten up every practice.

Most of these youngsters were not Division I athletes, but they loved the game. They courageously took punishment every day knowing they would not even get to dress for a game. I respected them for it. I gave a lot of thought to how I could get them to be competitive, perform their designated jobs as scout teamers, and let them have some success at the same time.

Everything is planned in organizing practice. The offensive and defensive coaches determine what they have to teach and the number of practices they have to teach it. I did the same thing with the scout team. I showed them films and made them learn the other teams' plays rather than run plays off cards. I could just call a play. That increased the number of plays they could run against our defense and would give the starters more repetitions.

I had to figure out something to improve morale, increase enthusiasm, and make a team that was physically outmanned more competitive. In our pre-practice meeting, I explained that we were going to score twice or make two big plays in each practice. I got some blank stares from them, but they were eager to know my plan. I just told them to be ready.

When Jimmy Johnson, the defensive coordinator, and Jackie Sherrill created the script for practice, they gave me a copy of the plays they wanted the scout team to run against specific defenses. The plays were usually numbered from one to twelve. My plan was to substitute a play I knew would be successful against a play on the script. When we went to goal-line practice, I decided this was the time to put the plan into action.

The ball was placed on the two-yard line and the script had second down and goal to go. The play we were supposed to run was 46 Power, a run play off right tackle. The defense had eight people in the box. I huddled my team. "Guys, this is it!"

They perked up and started clapping their hands and yelling. Everyone started watching them because it was unusual to hear that kind of reaction from them. Instead of 46 Power, I called a play-action pass off the 46 Power fake. The defense smothered the back we faked to on the play. Jackie started yelling, "Great job, great job." He celebrated too soon.

Our tight end faked a double-team block, then released to the corner of the end zone and was standing at the end line. He looked like the first guy out to practice. Our quarterback, Mike Fontanini, made a great fake, rolled outside of the contain man, and threw a perfect strike to the tight end. "Touchdown!" You would have thought we had just won the Super Bowl. The scout teamers sprinted into the end zone jumping up and down, hugging each other.

The defensive coaches were yelling at me, "That's not the damn play on the script! Run the damn play on the script!"

I said, "Sorry, I ran No. 6 by mistake." No. 6 was a play action from the four-yard line. We had a spirited practice after that, and the scout team played hard for the rest of practice.

After practice, Jackie Sherrill was fit to be tied. "Ray, what the hell were you doing out there?" Jimmy Johnson, in his wisdom, never said a word. I think he understood my motivation.

I responded, "Dammit, Jackie, don't you think letting these kids have a little success helps the defense get better prepared?"

Jackie retorted, "You are supposed to make those turds run what I put on the script."

That really pissed me off. "They're not turds, dammit! They are guys who come to practice every day, get the hell beaten out of them, and nobody gives them any respect. They might be turds in your eyes, but they are football players on our team trying to help us get better."

We got a little loud. The other coaches just observed—I think they enjoyed seeing Jackie upset. I said, "Look, most of these kids are never going to play. Most will never dress for a game and you want to call them turds? Just remember, they are our turds. So, I am asking all of you to not refer to them as turds anymore." Then I asked, "Didn't practice improve, and didn't they give you a better picture of our opponent after they scored?"

He could not argue with that because the scout team had really stepped up during practice. No one else in the room said anything, but I know they saw that the remaining time in practice went better.

In my next meeting with the scout team, they were all eager to know what we were going to do next to "kick their ass." They were my guys for sure now. I reminded them that we are all part of Iowa State's football team.

Jackie and Majors kept calling them "turds" after that confrontation. The other coaches quit using the term. Eventually, everyone stopped.

I did not subvert the script very often. When I did, there was some—but not much—objection to it. Eventually, my guys did improve. Some even got an opportunity to play on our special teams at home games. Success is the ultimate goal, but as Booker T. Washington stated, it should be measured by the obstacles people overcome in the process. This idea reflects an important concept about coaching.

Joe Avezzano and I were hired within days of each other and were about the same age. Joe was from Miami and played at Florida State. Coach Majors was always commenting on Joe's style of dress—nothing malicious, but we all got his drift. It is important to understand that Majors was Southern born and bred and quite conservative, so bellbottoms, platform shoes, and silk shirts were not clothes he would have chosen for his staff to wear.

Although I was not as extravagant in my style of dress as he was, I liked Joe. He dressed for the time. Joe was an outstanding line coach and a good recruiter. We both recruited in Florida and signed some great athletes to Iowa State.

Joe's family and I became friends. When I recruited in Miami, I ate a lot of real Italian dinners in his home. Joe and I shared a lot as friends and he got to meet and know my family in Ohio, one of his recruiting areas. We went in different directions when we left Iowa State, but we kept in touch until his death in 2013.

One incident defined our friendship during that first year. Our staff was attending the American Football Coaches Convention in New York. The convention started on Sunday and ended on Thursday. I was at the airport on Thursday to go on a recruiting trip to Miami when a voice over the PA system paged me to come to the Delta Air Lines desk, where I was told I had a telephone call.

It was Joe, who had left the convention on Wednesday to go to Florida to recruit. In a tone of voice I had never heard from him, he told me that Coach Majors had called and threatened to fire him.

The weekend before going to the convention, we had fifteen recruits on campus. Joe had three young men visiting from Cincinnati Moeller High School in Ohio—two black and one white. The two black athletes were outstanding players, but the white athlete was a five-star offensive tackle—a really top recruit. Joe, who had a great relationship with our black athletes, had two of our black athletes serve as hosts for the three recruits.

(*Above*) Greene's photo from a 1961 University of Akron football program. *Courtesy of The University of Akron Department of Athletics Collection, Archival Services, University Libraries, The University of Akron*

(*Below*) First high school coaching job with the Kenmore Fighting Cardinals, 1963. Greene is second row from top, on the right. *Courtesy of the author*

(*Above*) Greene while at the University of Miami, 1968. *Courtesy of the author*

(*Below*) Greene (*far left*) with his Florida and Georgia recruits for Iowa State University, 1970. *Courtesy of the author*

(*Above*) Iowa State University Football Coaching Staff, 1972. Greene is fourth from left. *Courtesy of Iowa State University Library Special Collections and University Archives*

(*Below*) Ad for Ray Greene's call-in radio show. *Courtesy of the author*

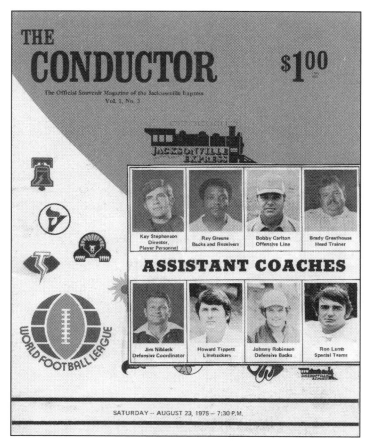

(*Above*) Souvenir program from Greene's time as an assistant coach with the
Jacksonville Express. *Courtesy of the author*

(*Below*) Greene (right) with the wide receiver group at Michigan State University,
1976. *Courtesy of Michigan State University Archives and Historical Collections*

(*Above*) The 1977 Michigan State University football staff photo. Greene is in the back row, second from left. *Courtesy of Michigan State University Athletic Department*

(*Below*) Greene presents a football clinic for women at Alabama A&M University. Bea Covington (center) diagrams a play, summer 1987. *Courtesy of the author*

(*Above*) Greene (*right*), Alabama A&M Athletic Director, and Paul Brand, Athletic Director at the University of Alabama Huntsville, renew cross town competition between the two schools. *Courtesy of the author*

(*Below*) Greene chats with players at Alabama A&M University. *Courtesy of the author*

(*Above*) Greene (*right*) with WAAY-TV in Huntsville preparing to broadcast the Division II National Championship Game. *Courtesy of the author*

(*Below*) Greene, a member of four Halls of Fame, shown here with one of the other recipients when he was inducted into the Huntsville-Madison County Athletic Hall of Fame. *Courtesy of the author*

Ray Greene, 2007. *Courtesy of the author*

Coach Majors' normal protocol was to meet, individually, with each recruit before he returned home. In meeting with the five-star tackle, he asked him how he enjoyed his visit. The young man told Coach Majors that he liked the school, but he didn't care too much for the parties he attended. He told Majors that he was going to go to Ohio State. Coach Majors assumed the young man meant he didn't like where the hosts took him, and he blamed Joe for his decision to have black athletes host a white player. I assured Joe that Majors wouldn't fire him because he was a good coach and a good recruiter.

We later found out that the young man had decided to go to Ohio State, but he accepted a visit to ISU only because of Joe. I told Joe, and later coach Majors, that we did not have a snowball's chance in hell to recruit that caliber of player from Ohio State's backyard.

Majors was not happy with me voicing my opinion, but he was a realist. Joe was not fired and he thanked me for having his back in the matter. Besides, the thirteen athletes he and I recruited that year played an integral part in helping ISU go to the Sun Bowl in 1971 and to the Liberty Bowl in 1972.

Another young coach on our staff was Jimmy Johnson. Jimmy would later move on to coach the Dallas Cowboys to Super Bowl victories and the Miami Hurricanes to a National Championship. He's now an analyst for Fox Sports. Jimmy is a fun-loving guy who enjoys a good laugh and is one of the smartest people I have ever met.

When we came to Iowa State, there was a revolution of sorts in collegiate athletics. Black athletes were protesting and demanding equal treatment and more black coaches. Many white coaches were in a quandary about how to treat and coach the new militant black athlete. It did not bother Jimmy at all.

I am not saying he was unaware of the evolving situation and individual differences but, when coaching and dealing with athletes on and off the field, he treated them the same. Because of that, he was respected by all of our athletes. During practice in the spring of 1969, my first year at Iowa State, there was an incident that defined Jimmy's style as a coach. Our scout team was running plays against the first-team defense. On a running play, the back fumbled the ball right in front of Steve Wardlaw, a black defensive back, who casually bent over to pick up the ball.

Wardlaw's lack of effort incensed Jimmy. In a dead sprint, Jimmy ran over, grabbed the ball and threw it about ten yards. He yelled at Steve to get his ass over there and fall on the ball. Practice stopped and everyone watched in complete silence.

This was the first real confrontation I'd seen there between a white coach and a black athlete. Steve started jogging toward the ball, but Jimmy ran up behind him and pushed him toward it. Steve went to the ground and scooped it up.

Jimmy took it from him and threw it forward again. This time, Wardlaw moved a little faster. This scenario continued three more times until Steve performed to Jimmy's satisfaction. Practice returned to normal.

Later in the staff meeting, Coach Majors and some of the other coaches seemed surprised that there was no negative reaction from the black athletes. I explained that players—black or white—accept good coaching, especially when they know they have executed poorly. Everybody saw that Wardlaw did not react like a winning football player. In a game, his feeble first effort in recovering the fumble might have led to a loss. You have to practice football the way you intend to play in a game. Even though the players and coaches all knew that, only Jimmy had the courage to dramatically make the point. His reaction helped to allay any concern that our coaches had about treating our black athletes differently from our white athletes as long as we were consistent and fair. It was a culture-changing moment.

Jimmy had a serious side, but he also had a great sense of humor. During a staff meeting on recruiting, Coach Majors ranted about how we had to do a better job of recruiting or all of our asses would be gone. Jimmy retorted by telling Coach Majors that we might be gone, but that the alumni would hang him up by his balls on the goal posts. We all cracked up as Majors stood there dumbfounded. He grumbled, "I don't think that was so damn funny, Jimmy." We composed ourselves and got back to the meeting.

King Block was the senior member of our staff. He was the first and only real cowboy I ever knew. We had a rodeo on campus and King actually jumped off a horse and bulldogged a steer. That was impressive, especially watching it up close.

King was old school and a good football coach. He had been a head coach at Arkansas State and taught me a lot about football. He did not have a problem with coaching black athletes, but he had some weird ideas about race. We often talked very frankly about it. He once said to me, "Ray, if those black folks living in the projects in New York and Chicago want to do better, why don't they pick up stakes and move to Wyoming (he had coached there) or Utah?" I could not keep from laughing. When I stopped, I told him he was crazy. I am not sure, up to the day he died a few years ago, that he changed his mind.

King had several black running backs among his players. One day after practice, he came to me and said he had a problem with Moses Moore, a young man I recruited from Miami's Jackson High School in Florida. I knew King rarely had contact with black athletes off the field and asked him what the problem was. He said Moses wouldn't talk to him. Although he had tried to talk to Moses in his office several times, it was always a disaster.

I asked him what he knew about Moses, and he became indignant. "I know he is a scholarship athlete!"

I then asked him if he had ever tried to learn anything about Moses's family, where he lived, or anything personal.

He replied, "I'm no damn counselor. I'm his coach and he's a football player."

I gave him a suggestion. "Why don't you try thinking of him as a young man first and see if that will change his attitude toward you?"

Since Moses was my recruit, King asked me if I would talk to him. I told him no—you're his coach and you're going to have to build a relationship with him. Two weeks later, King came to my office in an almost giddy mood. He talked about some personal things he and Moses had discussed and was excited that they were now talking regularly. We were making progress. Through the years King and I remained in contact until his death in 2014.

I worked for two head coaches at Iowa State—Johnny Majors and Earle Bruce. Both were outstanding coaches and each was very different from the other. John would often revert back to his Southern coaching techniques. He was an advocate of the "grab-em," "shake-em," and "jump on the pile" philosophy. I was enthusiastic, but not in the way that he wanted. You can't fake enthusiasm. Players see right through it. That is one of the reasons that Majors and I parted ways when he accepted the job at the University of Pittsburgh.

The proverbial straw that broke the camel's back occurred in the spring of 1970.

Two of my recruits from Miami were accused of raping a white student. When Coach Majors learned of it, he called me to his office to tell me that he was going to dismiss them from the team. This incident, he said, was a bad mark on his program. I was as much concerned as he was, and not only because of how it would affect the program. If they were guilty, my ability to judge the character of athletes during the recruiting process would always be in question.

I asked Coach Majors whether he knew for sure that the allegations were true. He told me that the young woman in question was the daughter of an important man on campus, and there was no reason for her to lie. However, black men have been unjustly accused of many tragic incidents because of lies told without a reason. One of many examples of this is the Central Park Five, who were found guilty of rape and later exonerated. I knew there was more to this story.

I cautioned him to wait until it was determined whether her allegation was true before dismissing the players from the team. Since John did not budge, I decided to find out more about what happened on my own. I called the players involved and asked them to meet me in the dorm boiler room at midnight.

My two recruits and four other athletes stood in the boiler room with somber looks on their faces. I was the first to speak: "I'm not accusing you of anything, but I need you to tell me the whole truth and nothing but the truth about the allegations against you. If you're guilty, I can't help you. However, if there's something I need to know that can help you, tell me now!"

They told me this story: One of them (my recruit) had been going out with the young woman making the accusations. He wanted to break up with her, but she kept pestering him. He came up with what he thought was a bright idea.

Before she came over to visit him, the other five guys hid out, in the dark, in his dorm room. The plan was that when he began making out with her, the rest of these dumb asses were supposed to come out and act like they were going to rape her. When the idiots came out, she was so frightened that she ran half-dressed from the room. According to them, no one—other than the player she came to see—touched her.

I asked them whether that was the whole truth. They said yes. I believed them, but was undecided about what to do next. There was a fact-finding meeting the next day with the dorm counselor, two students who lived on the floor where the alleged incident happened, the young woman, and me. The young woman claimed that all of the players raped her, but she seemed to be hiding something. She also claimed that she screamed repeatedly, but neither of the two people who lived on the floor or the counselor had heard anything.

The incident had allegedly taken place before exams nearly two weeks earlier. When asked why she had not told anyone until now, she replied that she was embarrassed. The meeting ended. When she left, the counselor said he would meet with her again the next day.

Late in the afternoon the following day, the dorm counselor came to my office. I held my breath. Apparently the father was unaware that his daughter was dating a black athlete. In addition, she had done terribly on her exams. She told her father that she did so poorly because she had been raped by the black athletes and could not concentrate on her studies leading up to exams.

She had broken down in the meeting with the dorm counselor and admitted the truth, which corroborated with what the players had told me. Word of the incident did not get out, since most of the students had left campus for summer vacation.

Coach Majors decided to suspend the players for the first three games. Although I did not say anything to Coach Majors, I thought the punishment was not sufficient. I later told the athletes what I thought. They were apologetic and appreciated me not judging them guilty before discovering the truth.

I thanked them but reminded them that there would still be consequences for their actions. I made them get up every morning at six to run the stadium steps and warned them that if they missed a day, I would ask Coach Majors to extend their suspensions for the whole season. When I realized that I had to share their punishment because I also had to get up early, I got one of my managers to oversee them.

What surprised me most during ISU's spring practice was that the players played better than they looked. Compared to the physical size of the teams in the Big Eight Conference, we were outmanned and lacked quality depth. Part of my job was to break down the previous season's game films. Looking at Nebraska, Oklahoma, Colorado, Kansas, and Missouri was a little scary. Oklahoma State and Kansas State looked similar to us, but each had a few big-time athletes.

The teams I mentioned, other than Kansas State and Oklahoma State, looked like professional athletes. Many became outstanding pros. We had several fine athletes on our first teams, but we had no quality depth. However, what we lacked in size, we made up in intensity.

There were no major coaching changes in the Big Eight after the 1968 season, so there would not be major changes in our Big Eight opponents' offensive and defensive schemes. I went through each film, charting the down, distance, position on the field, hash mark, formation, motion, ball carrier, yards gained, and defense. If it was a pass play, I noted the route and the result.

After completing each film, I wrote notes to be included in a scouting report. I then took the information to the computer center. They transferred it to punch cards and sent the report back to us. It was usually at least two or three inches thick. In the interim, I called the nonconference teams that our opponents played to trade films and break them down in the same manner. In addition to the film work, I had class papers to write, so I spent some long evenings at the football office and in the library.

Spring practice went well. We made progress, but we had a tough road ahead to make it into the top echelon of the conference. After spring practice, several pro scouts visited to look at film of our professional prospects. Because I was the quality control coach (a fancy name for the person who was in charge of films), I met all of the scouts and provided them with files and data on the players they wanted to see. Everyone was interested in Otto Stowe, a wide receiver who was projected to be drafted in the first to third rounds. The Atlanta Falcons showed the most interest and had the top pick because of their record. They had him projected as a first-round pick and we thought it was a foregone conclusion he would be a Falcon.

Otto was our best athlete by far. More importantly, he was a good student and classy young man. Like most of the black athletes at that time, he wanted to proudly assert his blackness. Otto, in his quiet way, did not participate in rallies or other activities. He did, however, grow a large afro. He was never boisterous, was a good student, and an outstanding wide receiver.

We thought he would be drafted in the first two rounds and were disappointed when Atlanta did not draft him. He was drafted in the second round by the Miami Dolphins, where he had a productive pro career.

It was not until the following year that I learned some disturbing news. The head of scouting from the Atlanta Falcons, Bobby Beathard, stopped by our office to view films of prospects. While discussing our prospects with him, I asked why Atlanta did not draft Otto. Bobby, who had just recently become the director of player personnel, told me he had asked the same question of his staff when they were discussing past drafts.

Otto had been classified as a "bad actor" by one of the scouts—not because he lacked talent or because he had caused anyone trouble during his collegiate career. In fact, he was an ideal student-athlete. The scout, apparently, did not agree with black athletes protesting their treatment, so he assumed Otto was part of the protests because of his hairstyle.

I wanted to call Otto but decided against it. Ultimately, he got to play on an undefeated Miami Dolphins team that won the Super Bowl. Atlanta was a long way from becoming a Super Bowl-winning team. But, I made it a point to tell every scout who visited us that story. Even though they all said it was a terrible mistake, I don't believe they were as sincere as they claimed to be.

CHECKING ON THAT PROMISE

Dan Robinson called during the second week of spring practice to ask whether I had arranged the meeting with the players and Coach Majors. Coach Majors had agreed, somewhat reluctantly, to meet with the Black Students Organization after spring practice. I told Dan that I would arrange the time and date and let him know.

During our daily morning meetings, Frank Randall, our trainer, gave the staff an injury update. Frank was a no-nonsense person. His job was to let us know who could and could not practice and give us the probability of which injured players would be ready to return to practice.

Though his report was normal procedure, I noticed there always seemed to be some concern, usually negative, about black athletes who were injured. A couple of coaches always seemed to doubt the veracity of Frank's evaluation of them. I said nothing but kept my thoughts in mind for the meeting with Coach Majors; he had dismissed the previous trainer because of his negative attitude toward our black athletes. Although he was in staff meetings, I felt it necessary to call his attention to what I observed. I started keeping notes during staff meetings, a practice I found useful and continue to this day because people don't always remember what they say, especially when they don't want to be reminded of it. I call it selective amnesia. Evidently, Coach Majors spoke with the staff because those negative comments ceased after Frank's morning reports.

RACIAL PROGRESS IN AMES

One of the perks afforded the coaching staff was free membership in the Ames Country Club. In 1972, the Elks Club in Ames still subscribed to a policy that denied blacks entry into their organization. Ironically, that chapter was one of the catalysts to help change the policy in 1973.

In 1971, the Elks invited the Iowa State football coaching staff to a dinner honoring us for our successful football season. When we were invited, I do not believe Coach Majors was aware of the organization's policy. We had a wonderful evening, and no one treated me with disrespect.

However, a couple of days afterward, one of our ardent supporters called me to say that several members had expressed some displeasure about me attending the event. Even though he was an Elks member, he was unaware of the policy. Being a well-connected businessman in Iowa, he promised me he would use all of his influence to change the policy. Several weeks later, he invited me to the club for lunch. The members made a concerted effort to shake my hand and welcome me.

Other than that incident, I always felt welcomed in Ames. Ames, Iowa, is a typical college town. I found it to be a great place to live during my five years there.

The university, at the time, had more than nineteen thousand students. Of that number, about 150 were black, including athletes. It was possible to walk around Ames for days, even weeks, and never see a black person.

The coaching staff and their wives often went to dinner at various restaurants and I don't recall ever seeing a black family while out for dinner. There were, however, several black families that I eventually met. All of them were professors, veterinarians, teachers, or in some type of business.

Some of the ones I knew were not interested in or happy about black student protests or anything to do with the new black pride movement. It was intimated to me on several occasions that they would rather be called "colored" or "Negro" than "black."

It appeared that some thought they could blend into the white culture of Ames without being part of the history taking place around them. The majority of the black people I knew did not feel this way. However, I made it a point to tell those who felt they could blend in that there was no escaping their blackness even in a serene, safe place like Ames, Iowa.

One evening at a party, I asked why one fellow, a veterinarian, had a bandage on his little finger. He said he cut his pinky doing a procedure. I broke out laughing and could not restrain myself from making a pointed comment. This fellow was as black as coal, so I corrected him by saying, "you mean your blackie, don't you?" He didn't say a word, but I made my point.

Meanwhile, ISU's Black Students Organization told me that they had a difficult time finding a faculty sponsor for their organization. Several white professors volunteered, but the students wanted a black sponsor. I asked Dr. William Bell, the Dean of Student Affairs, whether he would be the faculty sponsor for the group. He agreed.

Later, André Watts, the famed black classical pianist, came to campus to perform. Afterwards, the BSO invited Mr. Watts to come to their campus headquarters, named the "Black House," to speak with the black students.

However, some black faculty members refused to attend the session because they did not want to be associated with what they considered to be a segregated event. However, it was not a "black" thing. Several white professors and white students attended. Pat and I went and had a wonderful time meeting and speaking with a world-renowned artist.

OLLIE KELLER: ONE OF MY FAVORITES

I would be remiss if I did not mention one of my favorite coaches on our staff. Ollie Keller, who was a little older than the rest of us, coached running backs. He had been a successful high school coach in Tennessee. The first black football player at the University of Tennessee, Lester McClain, had played for Ollie in high school. Ollie and Majors were about the same age and played college football at the same time but at different universities. Majors played at the University of Tennessee and Ollie played at Memphis State.

My guess is that Majors hired Ollie because of his success in Tennessee high school football and the respect he had among the state's high school coaches. He was a good selection because he recruited several blue-chip athletes to Iowa State. Nothing fazed Ollie. He had retired from Tennessee high school coaching and I got the feeling he took the ISU job just for the fun of it.

One afternoon in the off-season the coaches, including Majors, were sitting around talking in good fun about who might have been the better athlete. The discussion ended after Ollie told John, "You should be glad I didn't go to UT." Majors asked him why.

"Because if I had gone to UT, your ass would have been sitting on the bench."

Everyone was surprised when John didn't protest Ollie's declaration. The only comparison that was available to judge John's and Ollie's athletic ability was what could be gleaned from playing basketball with them. At noon during the off-season, the staff played basketball to keep in shape. Ollie was definitely the better basketball player.

Later that same day, the evening news presented a story about a young man, Poindexter Williams from Fort Pierce, Florida, who had been killed in Vietnam. Several whites in Fort Pierce did not want him buried in the white cemetery where other soldiers were buried.

Poindexter Williams was a wide receiver on the football team when I coached at Dan McCarty. He was a good player, but he was a better person. He was well respected by his teammates and other students on campus. Although it was disappointing to learn that the racial divide was still alive in Fort Pierce, I was not surprised.

Dr. Floyd, my friend in Fort Pierce, gave me some details on what was happening. What he told me confirmed my belief in young people. A large group of Poindexter's former white classmates went to the Mayor and threatened to protest the decision to not bury Poindexter in the white cemetery. Their effort gave many of the residents the courage to join them, and in the end, they integrated the cemetery.

MODERATE SUCCESS IN THE FIRST YEAR

During my first year at Iowa State, we were close in every game but did not have the manpower to compete against most of the Big Eight teams. We won three games against our nonconference opponents and beat Kansas State and Oklahoma State in the conference.

A 5–6 record was not what we wanted, but the fans were really excited about the outlook for our football team. The dean of the department of education lived next door to me. He congratulated me on a great season every time we talked. When I reminded him that we had a losing season, he explained that it didn't matter because he had watched ISU play for twenty years, and this past year was the first time he attended a game expecting us to win.

Another reason he was so excited was the anticipation of the outstanding players moving up from the freshman team. The 1970 freshman class was hyped to be the best freshman class in Iowa State history. Of the thirty-nine players we signed, thirteen were signed by me and Avezzano. They had size and speed and proved they could compete in their daily battles against the varsity.

Coach Majors, on several occasions, asked me to speak at the local Quarterback Club meetings. Each time, the freshman team was always a topic of the members' questions. This group of young men would eventually give Iowa State the athletes it needed to compete in the conference. In the fall of 1970, while the varsity went 5–6, the freshmen won four of their five games.

We should have won all of them, but I got too smart for my own good. We were playing Nebraska. We took the lead in the fourth quarter and I made a dumb decision to try an onside kick, because on the two previous occasions that we kicked off, I saw the up-men running backward to block before the ball was kicked.

Evidently, their coaches saw the same thing and corrected the mistake. This time, they did their job and recovered the onside kick. They ultimately scored a touchdown and won the game 14–10. It was a learning experience, but it was still my dumb mistake.

Our fans were disappointed when they realized that we should have won, but not critical. The Nebraska freshmen were the ones we would be competing against for the next three years, and Iowa State had never come that close to beating a Nebraska varsity or freshman team in the past. Justified hope is a wonderful thing.

In January 1971, at the end of my second season as freshman coach at Iowa State, I went to the American Football Coaches Association (AFCA) Convention. While there, I heard the rumor that our defensive line coach at Iowa State was offered another position and had accepted. That meant there was an open position for the coach's job. I anticipated Coach Majors would consider me for it. He left the convention early so I called the office on Thursday, the last day of the convention, to speak with him about the opening.

Since Coach Majors would not be back in the office until the following Monday, I asked the secretary whether he had said anything about the defensive line job. To my disappointment, he had hired Jim Dyar.

Jim was a graduate assistant who had joined the staff the previous fall. Jim had played defensive line in college and had been a graduate assistant at the University of Houston before coming to ISU. He was more qualified than I was for the job. However, I thought it remiss of Coach Majors to not even inform me, a full-time staff member, that he at least had considered me but did not think I had the experience to be the D-Line coach. I could have understood that thinking.

I was so angry when I returned home on Friday that I decided to resign. I wrote my letter of resignation and waited patiently for our staff meeting on Monday morning. At the staff meeting, Coach Majors began talking and I interrupted him to ask whether I could have a minute to read my letter. He saw that I was dead serious and allowed me to speak.

I began, "I am resigning, immediately, from the Iowa State coaching staff. I have done a good job and will not have it taken for granted that I am just happy to be here. Considering the job I have done, I think I should have, at least, been considered for the position just given to Jim Dyar.

"Not extending that consideration is disrespectful to me and my aspirations as a football coach. I have no ill feeling toward Jim and understand that although I played defense, he has spent his total coaching experience as a defensive line coach. I sincerely wish you, him, and Iowa State Football the utmost success." I then handed the letter to Coach Majors.

There was a moment of silence that seemed like an eternity. Coach Majors broke the silence, stood, and told me to come downstairs with him to his office. Once there, he shut the door and sat down on the couch beside me. He usually sat behind his desk when he called anyone to his office. He could look down at them from there. This is a good technique to show who is boss.

He wondered why I hadn't asked to speak to him privately. I told him I thought the staff ought to know why I was leaving. He held up the letter, read it over again silently, and then tore it up.

"You're not going to resign."

"Yes sir, I am!"

Majors still wanted to let me know he was boss. He went on, "I do not have to tell you who I hire." Then, he relented a bit. "But you have a point. I didn't think you would be interested in that position, but I should have let you know that I considered you. And I did."

I wasn't sure if he was telling the truth, but I wanted to believe him. Since I had been there, he had always been straight with me. He repeated that he wanted me to stay and asked me what I was going to do. When I asked him to give me some time to think about it, he advised me to go home and talk it over with my wife and get back with him later.

Pat advised me to do what I thought was best for our family. Later that evening, I called John and told him I was still a member of his staff. On Wednesday, I flew to Atlanta to begin recruiting in Georgia and Florida.

In early April 1971, John called and asked me to come to his office. I had not been in his office since our last conversation in January. This time he was sitting behind his desk. He told me to have a seat. "The receiver job is open; do you want it?"

I replied, "What about Gordy?" Gordon Smith was the receiver's coach and a former pro tight end with the Minnesota Vikings. He said Gordon has been accepted into the FBI Academy and was leaving.

Just like that, I became the receiver's coach and had the opportunity to coach several of the players I had recruited. I don't know whether my act of resigning back in January had anything to do with his decision to offer me the receiver job, but I believe it did.

A few weeks later, John again exhibited his confidence in me. While I was recruiting in Memphis, Tennessee, he called and told me he wanted me to speak in his place to an ISU alumni and friends group there. Thinking it would be in a hotel or similar, safe venue speaking to a group of businessmen, I was taken aback when the event was an old-fashioned country cookout in very rural Tennessee not far from Memphis. When I finally got there and saw that I was the only black person among about 150 silver-haired white folks, my first thought was, "What am I doing here?" I could be lynched and disposed of and no one would ever know.

But these were Iowa State people. I had a great time, gave a nice speech. John told me later that the group spoke highly of me.

BEST SEASON IN SCHOOL HISTORY

In 1971, we had the best season in Iowa State's football history. We were 8–3 with the three losses coming at the hands of Nebraska, Oklahoma, and Colorado, who ended the season ranked first, second, and third in the nation in the AP Poll. We were invited to the Sun Bowl in El Paso, Texas, to play the Louisiana State Tigers. It was a wonderful trip for our wives, alumni, team, and their families. Best of all, our fans were going to enjoy the team's first postseason game in many years.

We had fun in El Paso; we bought cowboy hats, Tony Llama boots, and lots of other stuff. Practices were spirited and crisp and we were ready for the game. On the morning of the game, I heard the strangest pregame prayer. Most pregame prayers involve thanking God for the opportunity to play the game, safety for both teams, letting both teams play to the best of their abilities, and to let His Will be done. Our team Chaplin, Father LaShera, said all of those things but went a little further. He closed by telling God, "We need a victory and we ask that you help us in that endeavor." His prayer was not answered—we lost the game.

Of the thirteen players Joe and I recruited, six were starters when we took the field. The others were backups that played major roles. We lost the game 33–15, but our fans—starved for a good team and just happy to be in a bowl game—were elated. We became the talk of Ames and could not go anywhere without being congratulated by grateful fans who had stuck with the Cyclones through all of the bad times.

The only negative thing—other than losing—that happened at the Sun Bowl occurred during the game. LSU had no black athletes on their team. Several of their players made derogatory comments to our black athletes during play on the field. Since the game was played a couple of days before the AFCA Convention, I decided to address this at the closed coaches' luncheon meeting at the convention on Wednesday afternoon. No one knew that I was going to make a statement. I did not really know exactly what I would say.

The luncheon was for Division I coaches only to provide an opportunity to discuss issues affecting Division I universities. There were more than 1,500 coaches in the room, and all eyes were on me when I stood. I began by relating what had happened at the Sun Bowl, and I went on to tell them that there were no black head or assistant coaches represented on any committees or in decision-making positions in the AFCA.

In addition, I told them that I was only aware of one black coordinator in Division I football. This caused a stir. Charlie McClendon, the AFCA president who was conducting the meeting, was looking through the AFCA Journal to determine whether what I had said was true.

I had scoured the Journal before going to the convention, so I knew it was true. It was apparent that the issue had never crossed his mind. There was some discussion among the vice presidents on the podium. When they finished, they said they would look into the questions I had raised.

When the meeting ended, Penn State head football coach Joe Paterno came to me and expressed his dismay at what I had said, especially concerning the incident at the Sun Bowl. He told me that there was no place for that in college football and pledged to take steps to make sure it did not happen again. The result of my presentation was that the AFCA created an Assistant Coaches Committee and named a black coach to the Trustee Board.

Coach Majors seemed unhappy that I had spoken out at the convention. Nothing was said, but I sensed his displeasure.

In collegiate football, the path to becoming a head coach is well defined. First, you are a position coach. Then you move to an offensive or defensive coordinator. The next step is the head coach's position. For black coaches, the process was like a toll road with no money to pay the toll. By 1971, most football programs had a black assistant coach, but there was only one coordinator that I knew of—Frank Faulks. Surprisingly, he was a coordinator at the University of Arkansas, one of the last schools in the Southwest Conference to recruit black athletes.

Meanwhile, back at ISU, I was happy with my new position as the receivers' coach. Two of my three starters went on to successful NFL careers. However, I wanted to be a head coach and the manner that Majors had handled the defensive line coach's job still nagged at me.

After my AFCA speech, Majors' attitude toward me changed. Looking back, I believe he might have fired me were it not for my recruiting success and his notion that he might have an uprising among the black athletes. It was faulty reasoning, but it affected my recruiting.

Majors had rejected several athletes I invited to campus. All of them wound up at Division I universities and we had to compete against a few of them within our conference. I asked a couple of our coaches why they thought Majors had done that. I learned that he thought if too many of them were recruited from the same area, there might be repercussions if he had to enforce discipline on one of them. He feared they might all revolt. Because he saw them as a group and not as individuals, his thinking cost us some outstanding athletes. Let me be clear—although the majority of athletes I recruited were black, I also recruited several outstanding white athletes. None of them were ever rejected.

THE BLACK COACHES ASSOCIATION

Since I had spoken about a subject that was uncomfortable to some at the AFCA Convention, I felt I had to do something to ensure that other black coaches and I were given serious consideration when coordinator positions opened. The best way to do this was to try organizing black coaches to let head coaches and athletic directors know that we were not just happy to be assistants and that we wanted the opportunities to be head coaches. That meant first being considered for coordinator positions.

To begin, I called all of the black coaches I knew at universities in the Big Eight and Big Ten Conferences to invite them to a meeting at the next convention. I asked each coach I spoke with to contact his coaching friends and spread the word about the meeting.

I used the AFCA Directory to get the addresses of all the Historically Black Colleges and Universities (HBCUs). I wrote a letter to each head football coach inviting him and his staff to the meeting. I personally knew most of the coaches in the Big Eight, but few in the Big Ten and the HBCUs. I hoped they would attend my meeting, but I would have to wait and see.

On Monday and Tuesday of the convention, I approached every black coach I saw and reminded him of the next day's meeting. Some told me I had already spoken to them and said they were coming.

Wednesday evening at five-thirty, I sat alone in the parlor room I had reserved, waiting for the coaches to arrive for the six o'clock meeting. Soon people started entering the room in bunches. My worst fear was over—there would be an audience. Several came up to me to tell me they appreciated what I had done at last year's convention.

My speech went something like this: "Gentlemen, I asked you here because I'm concerned about us, black coaches, getting a fair opportunity to progress in the profession we have chosen. Three years ago, I became the first black coach at Iowa State and perhaps the first in the country to be hired by a major university's coaching staff. Since then, most major universities have hired at least one black coach.

"Now, I want the opportunity to become a head coach. What I have learned since then is that to move up in this profession, the route is through becoming a coordinator. Most every Division I Institution now has an abundance of black athletes who are making significant contributions to their programs. However, unlike their white counterparts, I haven't seen their success on the field gain them opportunities in positions within athletic departments on the campuses where they played and graduated.

"Our players tell me that they feel they are there only to perform, but will never be considered as graduate assistants or in other positions when they finish playing. I concur with their thoughts. I asked you to come to this meeting to discuss strategies that will give us a voice in the AFCA to change the landscape for blacks in collegiate athletics."

The first coach to speak was Eddie Robinson Jr. from Grambling State University (an HBCU). His dad was the legendary Eddie Robinson who broke Paul "Bear" Bryant's record for total number of wins. He began, "What position do you coach or are you just a token?"

Anger swelled in me but I remained calm. I never thought the HBCU coaches would resent those of us coaching Division I. "I coach wide receivers; do you have another question?"

"Yeah, how is this going to help us?" he asked, referring to coaches at black schools.

I was as remiss as I had been when I accused Coach Majors about not being considered for the D-Line job at ISU. I had not considered the feelings of black coaches at black universities. I should have anticipated this. I answered, "First, let me ask by show of hands, how many in this room would like to be head coaches someday and would like to have the opportunity to coach wherever your ability takes you?" Nearly all raised their hands. "Then, by organizing and forming a viable organization within this organization, whether you coach at an HBCU or at a predominantly white institution, we will have a voice and effect change that will be beneficial for all of us."

The more than 150 coaches clapped spontaneously. Someone said, "Where do we go from here?" I explained that first, we needed to collect names, addresses, and resumés of qualified black coaches. Then, we can make recommendations for candidates to serve on a steering committee. The committee could meet during the summer and develop a set of guidelines. That meeting was the start of the Black Coaches Association (BCA). In the ensuing years, the organization grew. Athletic directors now use it as one method to find qualified minorities to interview when positions open.

The word about the black coaches meeting spread around the convention and eventually got to Majors. Although we never really talked about it in depth, I am sure he knew the substance of the meeting. There is power in organizing. Martin Luther King's success in organizing people, black and white, caused much concern for those who wanted the country to go back to the old way of doing things. The BCA would prove to be just as helpful in collegiate football.

DEFERRING TO THE HEAD COACH

During football practices, Majors would get involved in the coaches' drills and act as though he knew what they were doing. Of course, when the head coach takes over a drill, you defer to him. I personally told my group of receivers to listen intently when he came over. Then, after he left, we would go back to what we were doing. Later, as a head coach, I never interfered in an assistant coach's drills. If I had concerns, I discussed them after practice.

This plan worked for me. For Ollie Keller, it was different. One afternoon, Majors went over to Ollie's drill and started coaching his players. Ollie and I worked near each other and I could hear their exchange of words. Ollie got upset when Majors started coaching the backs. He asked Majors, "Do you want to coach 'em or do you want me to coach 'em?" It got a little heated and Majors pulled Ollie aside so we could not hear the conversation. From the body language I saw, the conversation did not appear friendly. After that, I don't ever remember Majors taking over one of Ollie's drills again.

While playing at the University of Tennessee, Coach Majors was a tailback in the single-wing formation. He was a great player who could run, pass, and kick. However, his knowledge about receiving and the pro-type passing game was limited.

It is important to remember that the passing game as we know it today was not in vogue at that time. However, my experience coaching the Run and Shoot offense and visiting the Cleveland Browns' camps during my earlier years as a high school coach shaped my philosophy about reading coverages, running routes, site adjustments, releases, and other nuances in the passing game.

This was somewhat foreign territory for Coach Majors, who was enamored with Steve Owens, the great tailback at Oklahoma, and the I Formation running game. One afternoon, I was teaching our receivers different release techniques, reads, and route adjustments against zone and man coverage. Majors came over to my drill and took over. He told our receivers that he just wanted them to take off full speed and make whatever cut they were supposed to make.

In the staff meeting the next morning, I objected to what he had told my group. I thought I had made my case but, at the end, he told me to have them execute the damn technique exactly the way he wanted.

There are many areas in which receivers can always improve. One is "take-off" (Majors' term for releasing off the line of scrimmage). Another is blocking. Those were Majors' criticisms each time he talked to the receiving corps. These are safe terms to use, regardless of how little one may know about the finer points of pass receiving, because a young receiver can always improve in these areas. I know by studying literally thousands of feet of film and tape that most teams will score eight to ten more touchdowns a season if their receivers block downfield. Anyway, I thought I had done well making my point and told myself to make my case with him again later.

In the office later that same day, I went for coffee in the break room just past Coach Majors' office. While there, I overheard a phone conversation he was having with Howard Schnellenberger, then the receiver's coach of the NFL's Miami Dolphins.

Majors was speaking with Howard about the conversation we had had about route running during the staff meeting. I listened as long as I could without being discovered and went back to my office. A couple of days later, Coach Majors called me into his office. He started by saying he had thought about what I wanted to teach our receivers and he wanted me to continue what I was doing, because it made sense. Thanks, Howard!

Now that I'd become a full-time assistant coach, ISU turned into a great situation for me on several levels. I learned how to organize a football program from the ground up, I learned how to recruit, and I had the opportunity to work with experienced coaches. Most importantly, however, I learned the importance of handling little things before they become big things. It takes great effort to change the mindset of a program not used to winning. Iowa State was a bottom-dweller in the Big Eight Conference when our staff took the reins. In two years, we became contenders and went to two straight Bowl Games.

We were not on par with Nebraska or Oklahoma yet, but we had become competitive. There are many things about which Coach Majors and I had differing opinions. However, his ability to motivate, his competitiveness, his emphasis on the kicking game, his enthusiasm, and his work ethic are qualities that set him apart from many other coaches.

Our improvement and success at Iowa State had not gone unnoticed. Majors became a hot commodity and his name was mentioned for almost every head coaching job that came open. He denied any interest in leaving Iowa State but, some of us knew that he had accepted the head coaching position at the University of Pittsburgh. In December 1974, after losing to Georgia Tech in the Liberty Bowl, Coach Majors was officially hired at Pittsburgh.

During the time leading up to his selection, he was being courted by several universities. Many Cyclone fans, upset by the rumors, placed For Sale signs his lawn. There were ill feelings toward him among many of his formerly loyal supporters.

John had not discussed any of his plans to leave ISU with me. However, I learned later that he had spoken with several of the other staff members that he planned to take to Pittsburgh with him. I was not included. I found out he was leaving during our preparation for the Liberty Bowl in 1973.

While in Memphis for the Liberty Bowl, I got a call from Lou McCullough, ISU's athletic director. He asked me to come to his room at our team's headquarters in Memphis. (Lou and Coach Majors, to say the least, were never on good terms with each other.) McCullough told me Johnny was leaving.

He could not hide his animosity toward Coach Majors. Many of us thought that Lou wanted to be the head coach. He had been a successful assistant at Ohio State before coming to Iowa State as the athletic director. Listening to Lou talk about Coach Majors was uncomfortable for me, so I did not lend much to the conversation.

Although John and I were not on the best of terms, my loyalty to him and the opportunity he gave me would never allow me to be duped into saying anything derogatory about him—to Lou or anyone else. I had heard John say some things about Lou during staff meetings but until my meeting with Lou, I was unaware of the depth of the rift between them.

Lou and I visited for about a half-hour. Before I left his room, he gave me an envelope containing $1,500—my bowl bonus. Lou said John had given the other coaches their money. Just as he did when he hired Jim Dyar, John did not give me the courtesy of telling me that he was leaving.

I did not speak with Coach Majors again until he was invited to speak to the Huntsville Quarterback Club in Alabama while I was the head coach at Alabama Agricultural and Mechanical University (Alabama A&M) in 1980. However, we have never talked about the circumstances under which he took the head job at Pittsburgh. At this point, it would be counterproductive. I learned much from Coach Majors and have great respect for the man. I will forever appreciate the opportunity he gave me.

Chapter 5

Forty-Two Years in Coaching
Plenty of Great Stops

From my first graduate assistant job in 1962 to coaching the Tennessee Valley Vipers in the Arena Football League in the early 2000s, I've worked with a few players who became stars, and some coaches who became legends.

I have already mentioned Ted Hendricks, Johnny Majors, and a few others I've had the pleasure to work with. Several other players I coached went on to do great things.

As a player, honesty and fairness were what I wanted from my coaches. I reciprocated with my players as an assistant and head coach. I believe the players trusted me as a man and as their coach. I spoke to them man-to-man and valued their opinions. They knew they were always welcome to come into my office or call me to discuss any problems they might have at any time.

Coaching is teaching. The classrooms are the meeting rooms and the practice fields. The final exam to determine a coach's effectiveness takes place on Saturday afternoons in front of thousands of fans who think the price of admission gives them the right to judge and criticize. The process a coach goes through to become a good teacher takes time. It begins with learning everything about the game—offense, defense, and the kicking game. A coach must read books by successful coaches, visit with coaching staffs at other universities to discuss philosophies, request and study tapes from NFL teams and other universities, study psychology and learning styles, and read about and study the art of communication and group dynamics.

A term I often hear while watching television broadcasts of football games is *game management.* In its simplest form, it describes handling situations that arise during a contest.

Few understand the amount of time coaching staff spends talking about contingencies. Our staff named it the "What if and When do" situations. When do we try to block a punt? What if it is raining and we have a three-point lead backed up on our two-yard line on fourth down? When do we go for the two-point conversion?

These are just a few of perhaps fifty or sixty situations that might happen in any game. Good game management occurs when a staff has a well-thought-out plan for any situation. I doubt that the Seattle Seahawks had such a plan in the 2015 Super Bowl when, from the one-half yard line, they threw the interception that lost the game instead of handing it off to their great running back, Marshawn Lynch. I have no problem throwing on first down any place on the field. Situations dictate play calling, and sometimes it's a crap shoot. However, in critical situations, it is important to do what your team does best.

Quarterbacks are often mentioned as game managers. In actuality, it is the coaches' job, regardless of the level of play, to teach them to manage the game. As with all individuals, some grasp the concept better than others.

Some coaches have an innate sense of leadership. Others have to work at it. I had the good fortune to work with several coaches who were good leaders on some level. My experience with them taught me two things necessary to be a successful head coach: one, what I should do; and two, what I should not do. Every good coach has to be a master at teaching. However, no head coach can master all the skills to teach the proper technique for all positions. A head coach must hire assistants who are experts in their particular specialties.

I have a better than basic understanding of the techniques required for every position. Teaching those techniques is a different story. As a position coach, I primarily coached the quarterback and receiver positions.

Over time, I have discussed the nuances of those positions with some of the finest coaches in the country. I visited pro camps and universities who utilized the passing game. I attended many coaching school clinics and I often learned something that made me alter my teaching technique.

For example, as a high school coach, I attended a coaching clinic where Wayne Hardin, then the head coach at the Naval Academy, spoke about something he learned in their rival game against Army. Army did not have a running back who had the speed to get outside. However, Army had an All-America wide receiver, Pete Carpenter.

Carpenter never came to the huddle and got the nickname "The Lonesome End." Army would throw the ball to him on quick passes and let him go one-on-one against a smaller defensive back. He said Army used those plays as their sweep.

The ideal position for a skill player is to get the ball in open space where he has two ways to run. Hardin joked that it was just a longer handoff than it would have been had they given it to a halfback in the backfield.

That made sense to me, and we utilized the quick passing game throughout my coaching career. It has become a staple of the pro and collegiate passing game. I taught my position players several skills. One is a technique I taught Kirk Gibson at Michigan State. Kirk went on to become a great baseball player with the Detroit Tigers, Los Angeles Dodgers, and later was the manager of the Arizona Diamondbacks. He could just as easily become a great professional football player as a wide receiver. In his autobiography, *Bottom of the Ninth* (Sleeping Bear Press, 1997), Gibson described my coaching:

> [My] size and speed were great, but they still didn't stop me from getting "cut" during our home opener against Purdue. I caught a ball deep in Purdue's end of the field and began churning upfield, running over a couple of defenders on my way to the end zone. That's when a linebacker, Fred Arrington, torpedoed me with his helmet, right on the side of my shin bone. It was the first time I had ever been "cut," and I went flying. I hurt for three weeks.
>
> Ray Greene, our receivers coach, who had worked in the old World Football League, a few nights later taught me a little maneuver known as "The Flipper," which was designed to put the cut artists out of business.
>
> I would take the ball while running and cradle it in the arm opposite the defender's side. If he were coming low, helmet first, I would get down

just as low to intercept him, discreetly submarining my fist into either his solar plexus, beneath his shoulder pads, or square into his Adam's apple, which would leave him gasping for air.

While trying for the next ten minutes to find his breath, he could contemplate the wisdom of plowing his helmet into a man's lower leg. It was purely a survival tactic—one that ensured that if a tackler tried to cut me, he would pay for it.

Football is an intimidating sport, and you absolutely *must* be the intimidator. When I looked across that line of scrimmage, I knew I had to own the defender, physically and mentally, because when you've defeated him both ways, you have an edge. I call it the mental press.

The Flipper was just a new addition to my overall strategy: I wanted to punish a tackler, not illegally or unethically, but to the point where he would close his eyes. If I could get a tackler to close his eyes—believe it, most players close their eyes at contact—then I could make him miss and outrun him. And with those two advantages on my side a lot of big gains were guaranteed.

Kirk was one of many outstanding players at Michigan State and one of my favorites. However, whenever I think about the Spartans, one young man always comes to mind—Tyrone Willingham. Ty was an outstanding baseball player and also played quarterback on the football team. He was a senior when I arrived. He missed the first part of spring practice because he was playing baseball. We installed a new offensive system, so he was behind two other quarterbacks when he started practice. He was too good an athlete to not play, but I did not want to ask him to switch positions. I did not have to. He came to me and said he wanted to help the team as a receiver. That is the kind of person he was. Team success was more important to him that anything else. That type of attitude enabled Ty to advance in the coaching profession. He began at North Carolina State and eventually went on to become the head coach at Stanford and Notre Dame.

A NOTE ABOUT MICHIGAN STATE

Eight years passed between my time at Miami and when I arrived at Michigan State. Things had certainly changed. Michigan State had minorities at all levels in the university structure. The president, Dr. Clifford Wharton, was black and blacks held important offices in his administration. We had a black assistant athletic director, Clarence Underwood, who was later promoted to athletic director. Our equipment man was black, and we had three black assistant coaches. The head women's track coach, Nell Jackson, a former Olympian, was also black. I thought to myself, "The revolution is over."

One morning in a staff meeting, the day after Arthur Ashe won Wimbledon, I stood and jokingly announced to the staff, "Today, tennis; tomorrow, golf!" Everyone understood and laughed with me. I did not know at the time that I was being prophetic. It was one of those situations that Dr. Paul LeFavre, my philosophy teacher in college, spoke of in his class: sometimes people say something brilliant without realizing it.

Not long after I left Michigan State to become the head coach at North Carolina Central, Tiger Woods burst onto the professional golf scene. I called the football office at MSU to remind them about my prophetic statement. When Dan Underwood, one of the assistant coaches, recognized my voice, he said, "Dammit, I just knew you were going to call!"

We had a lot of fun as a staff at Michigan State and Iowa State. Most of the time it was either with our families or at various alumni gatherings; however, there were other times when we went out as a staff just to have a few beers and tell tall tales. At Michigan State, I contacted the assistant coaches of the teams coming in to play and invited them to go out with us to one of the local taverns after they got their players settled in for the night. (Most assistants spend a little time relaxing the night before the game—especially the young ones; personally, I made it a practice to be in bed by midnight when we had an afternoon game and never drank more than two or three beers.) I made an arrangement with the owner of one of the local taverns to provide free drinks to the opposing coaches. The owner informed us that they usually stayed very late, danced, and drank a lot of liquor. After all, it was free. In our pregame chatting, I noticed several coaches with red eyes—a clear indication that they had not slept very well. Was it ethical? I don't know. We all have choices to make.

GREAT ASSISTANTS DON'T ALWAYS MAKE GREAT HEAD COACHES

The Peter Principle declares that a person's upward mobility continues until he reaches his level of incompetence. In coaching, this happens all the time. An offensive or defensive coordinator does a great job in that capacity. His body of work earns him the opportunity to be a head coach. In two or three years, he gets fired.

There are many examples. Mike DuBose, after having a great career as a player and assistant at the University of Alabama, got the head coaching job there. It was a disaster and he was fired. Gerry DiNardo did a great job at Vanderbilt—so great that he got the head job at LSU. Three years later, he was fired. Nick Saban took over at LSU and won a National Championship.

Being a head coach is the same as being the CEO at a major company. To be successful, a head coach must have a vision of what he wants to accomplish and a well-thought-out plan to get it done.

More importantly, he must sell that vision to everyone associated with the program—administration, budget manager, assistant coaches, players, secretaries, etc. If there is anyone in his system that doesn't buy into his vision, disaster looms. Selling the vision does not mean everyone has to agree with him. In fact, he welcomes different viewpoints and disagreement, as long as they result in accomplishing the overall plan.

As the administrator of the program, the head coach is responsible for his program's success; therefore, he must involve himself in everything that happens—community relations, alumni coordination, players' academics, NCAA rules, setting standards of conduct, and anything else that affects the program.

Handling these responsibilities requires the head coach to hire staff he can trust and who have a degree of loyalty not required in most jobs. Because it is impossible for the head coach to be as close to his athletes as the position coaches, he has to have complete confidence in his assistant's ability to sell his vision and to do his job.

His relationship with players is one of communicating and selling his vision and then conveying the process necessary to accomplish it. Speaking militarily, the head coach is the general, the assistant coaches are the captains and lieutenants, the players who are team leaders are the sergeants, and the remaining players are the troops.

The others involved are the auxiliary support staff. The head coach must ensure that all remain in the loop. If he does not and one of the units fails in its responsibility, the organization will soon fail. Some coaches reach their level of competency as coordinators. Unfortunately, they get promoted to a head coaching position and, more often than not, fail.

As a head coach, I learned that having the dual role as athletic director doesn't usually breed success. One person can't effectively handle both positions. Managing ten or more sports is a job in itself. The head football coach needs to concentrate only on football.

I like to think athletes I coached responded well to me. There was only one incident in my coaching career where race might have played a role in my dealing with a player.

When I accepted a coaching position with the Jacksonville Sharks in the World Football League (WFL), we had a mixture of players just out of college and several who had NFL experience. Those with NFL experience were all good players who were nearing the end of their careers and saw an opportunity in switching leagues to get a few more big paydays.

Because of their experience, they were accustomed to the politics of professional football. Charlie Tate, my old mentor and the former head coach at the University of Miami, named me the offensive coordinator in Jacksonville. I planned the offensive practice schedule and ran the offensive team in practice. However, Charlie called the plays and I was in the press box feeding him suggestions. He usually took my suggestions.

Having never coached professional players, I asked Charlie for his suggestions on how I should deal with them. Some of them were older than I was. He told me to coach them as I have always coached—I would earn their respect if I could help them become better players.

I coached the receivers and tight ends. One of my players, Dennis Hughes, played at the University of Georgia and later with Atlanta Falcons. Dennis was a true Southern guy who spoke with a deep drawl, which made me wonder what he thought of me coaching him. He was a good player who early in preseason practice was the starter at tight end. I often talked to him about techniques he learned in the NFL and gathered some useful information. However, about halfway through the preseason, a young man, Keith Krepfle, who played for me at Iowa State, got comfortable with the system and started to compete with Dennis for the starting job.

By the time the season started, Keith had shown enough to beat out Dennis for the starting position. Incidentally, Keith, like Dennis, was white. In preparation for our opening game, I told Charlie that I was going to start Keith, and I knew Dennis would be disappointed being beaten out by a rookie. Though the difference in performance between the two was small, Charlie realized that Keith had made the most progress during camp and deserved the starting job. He agreed with my decision.

The week during preparation for our first game Dennis, who always had a lot to say, was not his usual talkative self. He gave me short answers when I asked him something, and he was not continually advising me on how to get the ball to him. I knew something was wrong. On Thursday, at the end of practice, I had Dennis come to my office after he showered and dressed.

I explained that I had sensed some anger and a change of attitude in him. He looked right at me and said, "Dammit Ray, you screwed me around. You cost me $10,000." Apparently, he had an incentive clause in his contract that would pay him $10,000 if he started the first game.

I was shocked. Evidently he read my reaction. "You didn't know, did you, coach?" I told him I had no idea about the players' contracts. I started Keith because I thought he deserved to start. "Hell, had I known, I would have started you, since I knew you and Keith would both play."

That satisfied him. He told me that it would have been tough playing for me if what he initially had thought were true. As he left, he turned and said, "Coach, I think you are as good a coach as I have ever played for. I had some reservations when I first came here and found you were going to be my coach. I'd never had a black coach and I didn't know what to expect. But I want to tell you I have great respect for you, and I'm glad we talked."

COACHING: STRESS AND PASSION

They say that working at a job you hate is called stress but working at a job you love is called passion. I loved coaching, and it can be stressful, but only if I let it. If a coach has a good plan and a process to implement it, the job should not be stressful. I jokingly tell people who ask me about the stress in coaching that I don't get stressed, I cause stress.

There is, however, some stress involved outside of coaching. When I became a head coach at an HBCU, the constant struggle with administrators to get adequate funds was, at times, stressful.

I had heard rumors that there were racial problems with some coaching staff. I can say without reservation that I never had a less-than-amicable working relationship with all of the coaches with whom I have worked. We had many open discussions about everything, including race relations, and I think my presence and contributions enabled them to better understand the problems that ignorance and racial stereotypes can cause.

I think when all was said and done, I did the best job I could in all my stops. If I was, in fact, making history, it is a history that will not be included in any publications other than this book. I did not let it weigh on any decisions I made. At the time, I did not consider it a big deal. However, looking back, it really was. I believe my entry into coaching on that level was one step forward in helping minorities advance in the profession.

The most important thing I learned about the business of coaching is that players at all levels expect a coach to be honest, have character, and help them become better players. Race is not a factor in that equation.

Since leaving the coaching profession, I have stayed in touch with many of the athletes I recruited and coached. Sometimes, they request recommendations for employment opportunities. However, more often, they trust me enough to confide in me concerning some difficult decisions they must make. Nothing pleases a coach more than to earn the lifelong trust of his players.

Coaches and teachers sometime fail to realize their impact on the lives of students. Fortunately, through social media and e-mail, I get lots of messages of gratitude from former players. Some of them call me from time to time to say hello and see how I am doing.

Recently, I attended a semi-pro football game between the Huntsville Rockets and Nashville Raiders. About midway through the second quarter during a timeout, I heard someone calling my name from the Nashville sideline.

The Nashville head coach was coming back to the fence, waving at me. He had called time out and asked his players to look into the stands. Then, he shouted, "Guys, that's my coach!" He said it two or three times until I waved to him to get back to work coaching his team. I was a little embarrassed because it called attention away from the game. I was also proud that he thought enough of me to do that.

The Nashville coach was Terrell Keith, a young man who played linebacker for me at Alabama A&M University. He was a good, dependable player whom I trusted because he did everything the right way.

He went to class, acted like a gentleman, and graduated from college. After the game, he told me he often uses many of the coaching methods he learned from me when he was a player. "Coach, I am not just talking about X's and O's. I'm talking about the importance of being honest with players and helping them become men who stand for something." He went on say that when former players get together, they talk about those things when my name is mentioned.

During my head coaching career, we won a lot of games and championships. We also shared some trying times. I would often tell our athletes that I loved them. Sound corny? Maybe so, but I really did. I loved them enough to demand that they do the things necessary to be successful people. Many times they bristled at my demands. However, I have learned that, as adults, they have come to appreciate the things I demanded from them. Knowing that former players talk fondly of me is like a gift that keeps on giving.

Former Alabama A&M Bulldogs football players have a Facebook page. Several of my former players talk about me on that page, describing me as a father figure, a great coach, a trustworthy man, and having a great mind for offensive football.

Their comments surprised me because I never tried to be their father. My goal as a coach was only to be professional in my approach and true to the pledge I had made to them and their parents during the recruiting process—that I would do everything I could to help their sons become good men, productive citizens and graduate from college. I made every effort to keep that promise.

DOING THINGS THE RIGHT WAY

I never spoke to our teams about winning because I believe winning is the byproduct of doing things the right way. What is the right way? A team member respects himself and others; he goes to class and studies; he cares about others; he cares about his personal hygiene; and, as an athlete, he strives to improve on some technique every day.

I assured our athletes and their parents that our coaches would do everything possible to prepare them. Whether we had won or lost, if they could look me in the eye after a game and honestly say, "Coach, I gave everything I could, " that was all I could ever ask of them.

I never compare myself to other coaches. However, I have studied other coaches, read their books, watched their games, watched their practices, and visited with them from time to time. I have learned there have been few great collegiate or professional players who have become great or successful coaches. Most successful modern coaches—such as Alabama's Nick Saban, Ohio State's Urban Meyer, Auburn's Pat Dye, New England Patriots' Bill Belichick, or the San Francisco 49ers' Bill Walsh—played football. But none were considered "great" players.

Football coaches are the ultimate teachers. Unlike classroom teachers, who give final exams at the end of each semester, football coaches are given a final exam every Saturday afternoon and receive either a pass or fail by the thousands of fans who feel qualified to grade them.

Some players are blessed with God-given physical talent that enables them to make the extremely difficult things appear easy. Of course, they work hard at honing their skills, but that only makes them better. I believe one of the reasons most great players who have tried coaching have not been successful is that they lack the understanding of why their athletes could not do some of the things they considered easy.

The coaches I named were good athletes, but each had to work hard on the little details and techniques required to play and compete. As coaches, they focused on coaching the details of technique and all the little things they had to do as players to survive. I was not a great player, so to be successful, I had to be a student of the game.

When I arrived at Alabama A&M in 1979, recruiting was over and I did not know the caliber of talent due to report for football the coming fall. I was pleasantly surprised.

One of the freshmen recruits was Dwight Wright. Dwight, a wide receiver, looked the part. He was thin and muscular and a handsome young man. I noticed he was very meticulous about the way he dressed on and off the field.

I had no immediate plans to play a freshman, but as practice progressed, I became more impressed with him. Even though he was not the best wide receiver we had at that time, he was very intelligent and made few mistakes. I had no choice but to let him break into the lineup because I could depend on him do exactly what was asked of him.

His teammates must have also noticed how he dressed and carried himself because they stuck him with the nickname "Broadway." Dwight became one of the top receivers to play at A&M and later was on the roster of the Buffalo Bills. Several years later, he was inducted into the Alabama A&M Athletic Hall of Fame.

Andre "Brick" Haley played linebacker at Alabama A&M. When I first met him, I told him that physically was he was not the type of linebacker I thought could play in our defensive scheme. He was short and had average speed, but during fall practice, he continually made plays. I could not keep him out of the starting lineup. Brick studied film, knew everyone's assignment and was a fierce competitor. Brick is now the defensive line coach of the University of Missouri and is recognized as one of the finest defensive coaches in the country. I believe what he has achieved in coaching, in no small way, resulted from what he had to do as a player to get on the field.

DISCIPLINE SHOULD BE ROUTINE

My definition of personal discipline is what you do when no one is watching. The legendary head football coach of the Green Bay Packers, Vince Lombardi, said: "Discipline is not a sometime thing." True discipline should be part of a person's everyday routine, both in football and life. With discipline comes success. Successful people take time to consider the consequences of their actions before making decisions. They don't always look for instant outcomes. Instead, they favor outcomes over time. They are willing to go that extra mile to be the best and, usually, when they get there, they find few others with them.

A successful person's word always means something. They take responsibility. They look you in the eye when they speak to you. They work until they get the job done. They earn the trust of everyone they interact with and never betray a trust. You know that they care by their actions.

Some young men grow up without fathers. I never tried to be a father figure, even though some may have considered me as such. I view that as the ultimate compliment. I treated players as my extended family and had no problem telling them I loved them enough to make them do the right thing.

Young people want discipline. They push the limits at times, but they want leaders to let them know when they've pushed too far. Success in football, unlike most other sports, involves eleven players at the same time thinking as one. If one player makes a mistake, ten others are affected.

I know, everything being equal, that the team that makes the fewest mistakes consistently wins. Football is a game of mistakes, so it is inevitable that even good players will make them. The difference between the good player and the average player is that the good player will make "new" mistakes. The lesser player will continue to make the same mistakes. It is the same with good teams and poor teams.

Lombardi also said, "Fatigue will make a coward out of you." A physically exhausted man is no good to anyone. He doesn't make things happen, he waits for things to happen.

I could not tolerate mental errors because they are a result of a lack of discipline and/or fatigue. Often, at the end of practice, when everyone was fatigued, we ran a team drill designed to improve mental acuity and stress the importance of overcoming fatigue. It is called the "the ten perfect play drill." The ball is placed at the ten-yard line. The teams (offense and defense) huddle, call their play, and run it full speed into the end zone.

We would run ten plays and each had to be perfect. No penalties, missed assignments, fumbles, etc. If a mistake occurred, we started over at play number one. Early on, the players were terrible. However, after several "start-overs," they eventually learned that even when physically fatigued, their minds could focus on the task at hand.

THE PHILOSOPHY COURSE THAT TAUGHT ME TO THINK

Earlier, I mentioned my philosophy teacher in college, Dr. Paul LeFavre. His course was an elective, and I had heard that it would probably be an easy A. It was not. Dr. LeFavre told us on the first day of class that once we proved we could think, we would ace the class. He warned us that people sometimes talk a lot and say something brilliant without realizing it. I did not get an A in the class, but I did earn a B for a paper I wrote.

As I recall, the paper had something to do with the 100-yard dash. My premise was that the race could never be finished if we kept halving the distance (50–25–12.5 etc.) until we got into an infinitesimal number. The reality is that we have seen runners finish the 100-yard dash and that, too, often, we confuse reality with erroneous facts that on some level, make sense. I still don't know what I meant. In other words, it was just BS. Dr. LeFavre said he agreed with me and called it a novel approach to thinking.

I was surprised, but I did not argue. I wrote another paper about football—not about blocking or tackling, but about football's relationship to living and life lessons. I mentioned topics like discipline, commitment, sacrificing individual accomplishment for the good of the team, etc.

I also discussed how I felt it contributed to my self-confidence and helped me deal with conflict on and off the field. Actually, I wrote the paper out of desperation because I could not think of another topic that would illustrate my thinking ability. Dr. LeFavre was impressed with how I had used football as a metaphor. He was also impressed at my outlook on life and how I was going to find my place in the world.

He told me at mid-semester that my grade was assured and that class attendance was no longer required. Still, I continued to attend. It was, perhaps, my most interesting college class. It helped shape my philosophy about teaching. Coaching, at that time, was not yet on my radar.

I learned later that Dr. LeFavre was a big football fan.

TEACHING AND COACHING

Fortunately, my first teaching job included coaching football at Kenmore High School. I found out that helping young people learn to think and work out their problems inside and outside the classroom made them better students. When they believe you care about what happens to them, they trust what you tell them in the classroom and on the playing field. When you establish that trust, students and athletes will work hard to please you.

What I had learned from coaches with whom I have worked helped me to become a successful head coach. Not everything I learned was positive, but the negative experiences taught me what not to do. For example, I learned the following: never presume a player wants what you want; never denigrate a player; be slow to judge; and never make rules you can't enforce.

Jimmy Johnson was as tough as a coach could be on his players. I think some of them probably hated him during practice. However, every day his players would drop by his office just to talk to him and not always about football. That's because they trusted him.

With Jimmy, what you saw was what you got. People, in general, respect that. It never surprised me that he was a very successful coach on the collegiate and professional levels. Athletes at any level respect a coach they can trust. Once an athlete trusts a coach, the coach can help the athlete become better at what he does.

I am not sure whether a person can be taught how to be that kind of coach. Most coaches know the X's and O's of football. Most are organized. Most have played and most have studied the psychology of coaching. However, few have that innate ability to connect with players in a special way. In basketball, there are many great players. There are only a few Larry Birds, Magic Johnsons, or LeBron Jameses. The same goes for coaches.

Chapter 6

Coaching Favorites

I've coached football at the youth league, high school, collegiate, and professional levels. Each had its advantages and challenges. At each level, there were young men at different stages of development who wanted to become better football players.

Working with young men provided me an opportunity to help them become more productive adults and better athletes. I found it amazing that many of the men I coached in professional football had never had a really serious discussion with their former head coaches about their lives.

I have recruited young men from different backgrounds, abilities, and aspirations. My goal as their coach was to help them enhance their abilities, socially and athletically, and provide them the tools to handle the disappointments and successes they would face in the future.

One of my favorite recollections from my coaching career involved Darryl Rogers, the man chosen to lead the Michigan State Spartan's football team in 1976. Darryl had been a successful coach at San Jose State. He was laid back and seldom got excited...

He understood the passing game and had just the right demeanor to coach and teach that type of offense. Today, they call it the West Coast offense. There was a level of comfort between him, the players, and the coaches. His level of confidence in what he taught not only kept the players loose, it got them to play with the same confidence. They were not afraid to make a mistake.

During a team meeting, after we had won a game we likely would have lost had we played a better team, he calmly told his players: "Football is a game of mistakes and the team that makes the fewest mistakes usually wins. This afternoon, we made some of the same mistakes we have been making. I know you're going to make mistakes, but to be a championship caliber team, you can't continue making the same mistakes. Make some new ones." It was subtle, but coaches and players got the message that we have to keep improving.

THE HBCU EXPERIENCE

In my career, I have had the opportunity to coach at four HBCUs (historically black colleges and universities), including North Carolina Central University, Jackson State University, Alabama State University, and Alabama A&M University.

When I left Michigan State to accept a head coaching position at North Carolina Central, I was unaware of the problems that now seem endemic to some historically black universities. It is difficult to describe the differences in major college football and black college football, but here's one example.

In a pregame meeting, one of my high school coaches made a statement when we were about to play the No. 2 team in Ohio: "Men, they are a good team—maybe a great team, but they put their pants on the same way that we do." A teammate whispered to me, "That may be true, but their pants are five sizes larger than ours." That analogy perfectly compares HBCU and Division I football.

A good friend of mine, Bob Lee, advised me not to take my first head coaching job at an HBCU. Bob is now a businessman, but he had a long and distinguished coaching career at the Division I level. His father was a former president at Florida A&M University, and Bob got his start at an HBCU. When I asked him why I should not leave East Lansing, Michigan to become the head coach at North Carolina Central, he could not give me a definitive answer. I took the job.

It did not take long for me to understand. Central was a Division II University in 1978. Academically, it was a match for nearby Duke University. Central has a beautiful campus and was the first HBCU to have a law school. At one time, John McClendon was its legendary basketball coach and many give him credit for inventing the Four Corner Offense that the University of North Carolina's Dean Smith made famous.

Dr. LeRoy Walker, the track coach, was a former Olympic track coach and one of the most respected men in track and field in America and worldwide. The football program was different.

I was told when I interviewed for the job that we would have the sixty scholarships allowed for Division II schools. When I got to campus, that number changed to forty-five. Our whole office was housed in the one room in the basement of the basketball arena.

In examining the football equipment, I found a mess. The practice equipment was so limited that I called Troy, the equipment manager at Michigan State, to ask him if he would send me some equipment. He agreed, and about a week later, a big shipment of shoulder pads, helmets, pants, and jerseys arrived, but they were all Michigan State colors—green and white. Central's colors are gray and maroon, but you to do what you have to do.

The players were the best thing about our program. We did not have a lot of talent, but they were a great group of young men. None of the athletes had experienced a winning season since they left high school, and they were filled with anticipation of a new staff turning things around.

At our first team meeting, there were forty-eight players and a few walk-ons. I gave them an overview of our plans and introduced our staff. I was only permitted to hire two coaches and was fortunate to find the coaches on staff were very good.

Robert "Stonewall" Jackson was the line coach. He had played at Central and later with the New York Giants. Jack was a neat freak. Every morning, when he came to the office, he polished his desk and straightened things up before he sat down.

He had many good stories. For example, one morning he was talking about his time as a running back with the Giants. Jack said that when he was a rookie, he bought a case of aspirins and distributed them to the defensive team. When I asked him why, he said the aspirin would take care of their headaches after they tried to tackle him.

Jack was in his sixties and looked as if he still had a few plays left in him. Jimmy Carter (not the former US president) was a defensive coach.

The two holdover staff members were graduate assistants. The coaches I hired were Bud Asher and Woodrow McCorvey.

Bud was my defensive coordinator. He later became the head coach of the Jacksonville Sharks in the World Football League. Woodrow "Woodie" McCorvey's only experience was as an assistant coach at Tate High School in Pensacola, Florida. I met Woodie at the American Football Coaches Association Convention. He was distributing resumés trying to get into college coaching.

I took his resumé and put it away to study it later. That evening, I got a call from Jim Dyar. Jim was then coaching at the University of Tennessee and recruited in the Pensacola area. Jim told me Woodie had asked him to call on his behalf and that me he thought Woodie would make be a great addition to my staff. It always goes back to who you know and who knows you.

Jim Dyar was a man whose judgment I trusted implicitly. I called Woodie and offered him the job—my first hire as a head coach. By the time the season began, I was so impressed with his work that I named him my offensive coordinator.

Through the years we worked well together, and his value to me increased. He was a good family man, an excellent teacher, loyal, and an outstanding recruiter. He had a great relationship with our athletes and everyone we had to deal with.

Woodie went on to coach at Clemson, the University of South Carolina, Mississippi State, and Alabama, where Gene Stallings named him assistant head coach and offensive coordinator. He is now an assistant athletic director at Clemson, where one of his former players at Alabama, Dabo Swinney, is the head coach.

I received outstanding cooperation from the faculty, student government, and our alumni, but not so much from our administration. We did not get our game uniforms in time for the first game, and funds were not available for our players to stay in hotels for away games. When we had to stay in dormitories on the campuses of our opponents, it felt like a throwback to when segregation denied blacks accommodation in motels or hotels. In spite of it all, our players played about as well as they could play.

In my first game as a head coach, our players had to wear practice gear of mixed colors because of an administrative holdup in processing purchase orders.

Late in our season, the rumor surfaced that Central was considering moving up to Division I-AA. I approached University Vice President Dr. S. Dallas Simmons, my boss, to ask whether the rumors were true. He said that they were.

Remember, we were not able to afford all the scholarships for Division II; our facilities were poor; our recruiting budget was limited. When I told the administration that we needed more scholarships, the president asked me, "Coach, why do you need more players? You can only play eleven at a time." At that moment, I decided to leave Central.

The move to a higher division would be a disaster. Plus, I was not given the courtesy of discussing the move with them before it happened. Two weeks later, I got another call from Jim Dyar. A friend of his, a banker in Huntsville, Alabama, told him that Alabama A&M had a head coaching vacancy. His friend was on the University's Board of Trustees and wanted to know whether Jim could recommend a black coach who had Division I experience.

So, Jim recommended me. He told me that Huntsville was a progressive city in north Alabama. However, the name Alabama had such a bad connotation that I had second and third thoughts about going there.

During my time at Iowa State and Michigan State, I recruited Florida and Georgia. I would fly into Atlanta, rent a car, and head south to Florida on I-75. Leaving Atlanta, I had to pass the direction sign that read "I-20" with "Alabama" underneath. It never crossed my mind to take that road. Now, I was going there to be the head football coach at Alabama A&M University.

Of all the coaching stops I have made, being head coach at Alabama A&M was my favorite. It was also the most frustrating and disappointing. Alabama A&M is located in one of the most progressive cities in America—Huntsville. It is a great place to raise a family, earn an education, and get a high-paying job. NASA has a huge presence in Huntsville. More importantly, people there are friendly and have respect for one another.

It is an ideal environment for a football coach. A&M is located within two hundred miles of several major population areas that are great recruiting areas such as Atlanta, Georgia; Mobile and Birmingham, Alabama; Jackson, Mississippi; and Memphis and Nashville, Tennessee. We never had a problem recruiting quality athletes. More importantly, the students receive more personal attention than at universities with thirty to fifty thousand students.

I inherited several great players, including Mike Williams (Washington Redskins) and Howard Ballard (Buffalo Bills and Seattle Seahawks), who became All-Pro athletes. Several others had the chance to play in the NFL or other professional leagues.

More important, though, they all got degrees. A great number of athletes not only received degrees, but also moved on to professional positions outside of football.

Still, it was a constant battle to get little things done for our program. We did not have decent practice facilities or our own stadium. Alabama A&M teaches students from around the globe the science of agriculture, yet we didn't have state-of-the-art practice fields. My questioning was not appreciated.

We had a lousy weight room, making it difficult for our athletes to gain strength and weight, and we had no input into their dietary needs.

Registering for classes was an ongoing problem each fall. Although the athletes were on campus weeks before other students arrived, our players could not register early. Freshmen could only register when the rest of the students arrived. Because of this, several had to miss practices to get the classes they wanted. Some of the major classes were scheduled at four p.m., forcing athletes to miss practices on some days.

This would never occur at major institutions. Still, in spite of the HBCU disadvantages, we prevailed. It allowed our athletes a valuable lesson— the necessity, at times, of having to overcome adversity to succeed.

I had the opportunity to coach at four HBCUs and three Division I institutions. Attempting to compare the difference between them would not be fair because of the circumstances from which each evolved. Segregation, lack of funding, poor alumni support, and other resources were the culprits. In spite of this, statistics show that although more black students attend predominately white institutions, more black students graduate from HBCU institutions.

However, I have seen many improvements over time at HBCUs, but not to the point where they can compete in the higher levels of Division I. Most HBCUs now have basketball arenas instead of gymnasiums, better practice facilities, and so on. When I coached at Alabama A&M, we played and beat Central Florida. Now, Central Florida's program in the last few years has been ranked among the nation's top programs in Division I football. The difference lies in the availability of resources and a commitment to excellence. With the same type of resources and commitment, there is no reason A&M could not make similar strides.

The major institutions are worlds apart from HBCUs in terms of resources. I think having the experience in both made me a better coach. Every situation is a learning experience. I made an all-out effort to incorporate the things I had learned coaching in Division I football into our program at Alabama A&M and I met a lot of resistance. I believe people naturally resist change and my persistence in trying to change things at Alabama A&M did not sit well with the powers that be. I felt as if they were asking, "who is this Yankee from the north coming in here trying to upset the status quo?"

When I left Alabama A&M, we had a winning program built by our coaches recruiting talented athletes with good character who were taught to understand the importance of hard work and sacrifice. When I left the program, in spite of the difficulties, the Bulldogs had won several championships and a built a solid foundation for future success.

Chapter 7

Regrets, I've Had A Few

I believe life is a series of choices and that you should use all the tools you have to make choices. To look back and second-guess the choices you make is unproductive.

I do have a few regrets, such as quitting piano lessons to concentrate on sports. Though I'll never know how good a musician I could have become, I know that making the choice to pursue sports allowed me to be my best self. Had I had stayed with music, I would not have had the opportunity to meet the wonderful people I met during the last forty years or enjoy the many great moments I have experienced as a player and coach.

Outside of my children being born, I can't imagine any better feeling than being on the sideline coaching in a game against the No. 1 team in the nation, or watching Kirk Gibson streak down the hash marks to catch a touchdown on a play we worked on all week in preparation for Purdue.

I have seen every major football venue in America and watched, coached, or competed against some of the finest athletes and coaches in the history of the game. I have seen young men break down and cry after losing a game where they played so hard they could hardly walk off the field. I have seen the same young men regroup and work harder in preparation for the next week's game. As coaches, we deal with the best of young men, and I know we make a difference.

To say I have regrets about not taking certain coaching positions offered to me would dampen all the excitement and positive relationships I have enjoyed with the players, coaches, and others with whom I worked through the years. Being a football coach enabled me to be my best self.

THE JOBS NOT TAKEN

In the spring of 1974, after Coach Majors left for the University of Pittsburgh, I was without a job. I expressed interest in the head coaching position at Iowa State and was granted an interview. Interviewing for a head coaching position in what was then the most prestigious conference in America was a really big deal.

I knew the ISU interview was just a courtesy, but I was going to make the most of the opportunity. Upon reflection, I realized that Iowa State or any other major university was not ready to hire a black head coach during that time in history.

During my interview, I told the committee that ISU had a unique opportunity to change the dynamic and history of collegiate football by hiring me as head coach. More importantly, the publicity would put Iowa State into the national spotlight and enable us to recruit athletes who previously might not have been considered.

I believe ISU missed a great opportunity. They could have been a great national program and contend in the Big Eight Conference. Since then, they have struggled in the middle of what now is the Big Twelve Conference. Though I didn't get the job, I got a call from a member of the interview committee, who told me I had impressed the panel during the interview, but the committee decided it wanted someone with head coaching experience.

Even though I told him I appreciated the call, I was really pissed off. Johnny Majors did not have any head coaching experience when ISU hired him. I had proved I was one of the best, if not the best, recruiter on the staff. The majority of the players I had signed during my first year became starters as sophomores. I was an accomplished public speaker. Coach Majors had let me substitute for him several times when he was unable to handle some of his speaking engagements. My ability to coach was never in question and several of our athletes, black and white, endorsed my candidacy. The players' support should have been an important consideration. The coach they chose was Earle Bruce—a good choice. I knew Earle from when

I lived in Ohio. He is an outstanding coach, and I was eager to speak with him about remaining at ISU on his staff.

In the two weeks following the Liberty Bowl, I had received calls from two Big Eight coaches offering me assistant coaching positions. Both were aware of the recruiting job I had done for Iowa State. I had made it a point not to be labeled as a coach who recruited only black athletes. The coaches who called me knew I had signed several white athletes their assistants had tried to recruit. I evidently had earned the reputation of being able to coach and recruit athletes of all races.

Fortunately, Earle reported to campus before I had to make a commitment to one of the other schools. He interviewed all the coaches who did not go with Majors to Pittsburgh. He retained Frank Randall, the trainer, and me.

Earle Bruce and John Majors were alike in their intensity on the field. Both demanded a lot from the players and both believed in coaching the "little things." Both men were strict disciplinarians and demanded nothing less than maximum effort and they both had the respect of their players. I know John cared. Even through the turmoil happening when I first interviewed and afterwards, the athletes never spoke negatively about Coach Majors. I think the players felt Earle's manner of expressing how he cared was different from John's. When Earle was head coach, there seemed to be a closer bond among the players and the head coach. Coach Majors just had a different manner of expressing the way he felt.

In 1973, Iowa State went 4–7. Our staff got along well and it was another learning experience for me. Earle's philosophy of offense was much like John's. He was an Ohio State guy and subscribed to the Woody Hayes philosophy of running the football. He would eventually be the head coach at OSU after Woody retired. The passing game played a bigger role in our offensive thinking than it did with Majors; however, I felt I needed a change if I wanted to expand my opportunities as a coach. So I decided to look for another job.

THE WORLD FOOTBALL LEAGUE

When the World Football League (WFL) was established, Bud Asher, the new head coach of the Jacksonville Sharks, called me in January 1974 to ask whether I wanted to coach with him. Bud was an attorney and judge in Daytona Beach. He owned two hotels and coached high school football there. He also coached at Bethune-Cookman College, a predominately black institution.

Bud was a fiery little guy. He went to college at the University of Georgia and was a friend of Al Davis, the owner of the NFL's Oakland Raiders. Because of his friendship with Davis, he had several pro contacts. He did not play football at Georgia but knew all of the coaches and learned football from them. I told Bud I would be happy to work with him.

Bud's life is emblematic of what America is supposed to be about. He told me about how he got hungry one night and there was no place close to campus to eat, so he got the idea to start what we now call a food truck. He borrowed some money from friends, bought a cart, made sandwiches in his room, and began selling them to students on campus. Eventually, he had several carts and employees. His business boomed. He got into real estate after college at just the right time and made so much money that he was able to buy the two hotels on Daytona Beach.

I left Iowa and moved to Florida to take the coaching position with the Jacksonville Sharks of the World Football League in February 1974. We held preseason camp in Daytona Beach to begin planning for the WFL's inaugural season. We had a great coaching staff that included Charlie Tate, my former boss at the University of Miami; Jim Niblack, a former Florida assistant; Howard Tippett, who went on to coach twenty years in the NFL; Johnny Robinson, the Hall-of-Fame safety who played for the Kansas City Chiefs; and Kay Stephenson, who would go on to become the head coach of the NFL's Buffalo Bills. I felt very fortunate to be part of an outstanding group of coaches.

Practice was going well and I was enjoying coaching professional athletes when I received a call from Alonzo "Jake" Gaither. Coach Gaither was a legend at Florida Agricultural and Mechanical University (FAMU). He had retired from coaching and was now the athletic director.

Most of the predominately black universities had the designation of A&M (Agricultural and Mechanical), A&I (Agricultural and Industrial) and A&T (Agricultural and Technical) after the state in which they were located. These schools were mostly in southern states, and they were initially created to train blacks in those fields and maintain segregated white universities. The accepted wisdom then was that blacks, in general, were only suited to those kinds of jobs. It wasn't true then or now, but at that time many white people thought it to be.

Gaither was an assistant at FAMU in 1938 under Dr. William "Big Bill" Bell. Dr. Bell was an All-Big Ten and All-American tackle for The Ohio State University from 1929 to 1932. Dr. Bell, who I had met while at Iowa State, was instrumental in helping me get hired there.

Dr. Bell led FAMU to its first National Black College championship in 1938, and again in 1942. Not long after he left FAMU to join the military in 1943, Gaither became head coach. Gaither went on to achieve the highest winning percentage in college football history (.844) at FAMU, according to the National Collegiate Athletic Association (NCAA).

I first met Coach Gaither at the AFCA convention in 1969. I'd just recently been hired at Iowa State. I introduced myself to him and he gazed at me with his steely eyes and said, "You are that boy they hired at Iowa State!"

I was not offended when he called me "boy" because older black men often addressed younger black men that way. It was not a derogatory use of the word. I even use it now in addressing some black youngsters.

"You have a terrific opportunity," he continued. "You are a leader, so be a leader!" I was stunned, first of all, because he knew who I was and second, because he gave me a direct order. It was like a father giving his son some stern and important advice. He and I would cross paths at future conventions, and he would always give me "the look" when we shook hands.

FAMU is an outstanding university; because I had taught, coached, and recruited in Florida, I was well aware of their academic and athletic excellence. Florida always has a great pool of athletes. Most of the black head coaches and teachers in Florida's segregated high schools graduated from FAMU and greatly supported the program. Recruiting was never a problem because, in Gaither's time, schools like the universities of Miami, Florida, Georgia, Alabama, and Florida State University did not recruit black athletes or students.

Recruiting at FAMU, then, was more a matter of selection. When I coached high school football in Florida, the National Letter of Intent signing day was in May. From the end of the high school football season until the first week in May, there was a steady stream of coaches from various universities on our campus.

They reviewed film, visited the homes of athletes they wanted, and did everything they could to persuade athletes to sign with them. No coach from FAMU or any HBCU showed up on our campus before the end of April. They never had to go through the recruiting process because they never had to compete. Were it not for integration, nearly all the great black athletes would be at FAMU, Grambling, Southern, Alabama A&M, Alabama State, or other HBCUs. Things had changed!

Today, the once-all-white universities are achieving great success in large part because of black athletes who previously were not welcome at their universities now dominate their programs. However, integration at those schools was gradual.

For the HBCUs, as the big schools started to recruit black athletes, their athletic programs and facilities, already in poor condition, would deteriorate further. The large stadiums and shiny amenities at the big-time universities attracted athletes of all races.

Why would Jake Gaither, the legendary coach who invented the Split T offense and conducted coaching clinics with legends Paul "Bear" Bryant, Frank Broyles, Woody Hayes, Darrell Royal, and Adolph Rupp, be calling me?

He wanted to know if I would like to be head coach at Florida A&M University. My first thought was what an honor it would be. My reply was sure, but why me?

He had followed my progress through the years and thought I would be a good fit for the university.

I asked him: "Coach, you have several assistant coaches who have been with you for many years who are good football men and obviously have done a great job. Why not one of them?"

He told me that I had established a great background in a good conference, that I knew how to recruit, and that I had excellent contacts within the profession. Besides, Dr. Bell, at Iowa State, thought I would be comfortable working with white people. Jake did not mince words. He knew what he wanted. I thought that was an odd statement, since FAMU is a historically black institution. When I addressed that point he said, "We're in the same city (Tallahassee) as Florida State and we need the support of the white community to be relevant when we ask for more funding. This job is bigger than just being the head football coach. Making a good impression with the press and working with community groups is going to be necessary to continue having a quality program. I believe you can bring in some fresh ideas to accomplish that."

The salary was in the $35,000 to $40,000 range. That was a lot of money in 1974. I would get the use of a car, a housing allowance, and a $100,000 life insurance policy. There were other perks that he said we could work out in the five-year contract.

"How many assistants can I hire?" I asked.

"Two," he answered. He also indicated that I would be required to retain the other assistants already on staff.

That put up a red flag for me. I asked, "Wouldn't hiring me create some resentment among staff who helped you build the program? I'm certain some of them thought they would get the job when you retired."

Gaither told me they did not have the experience I had and the kind of exposure needed for what he envisioned the program to become.

Not being able to hire my own staff was a dealbreaker for me.

The call from Coach Gaither came on Wednesday, and he needed an answer by the end of the week.

I spoke with Bud Asher, Earle Bruce at Iowa State, and my wife. They all thought it would not be a good move for me. I called Coach Gaither Thursday evening to decline the job. When I explained why, he actually told me that he probably would have made the same decision if he had been in my position. His words meant a lot.

FAMU is a state university. Every time Florida State got something new for its program, FAMU would get the same. Rudy Hubbard, another Ohio State guy, was eventually selected to be FAMU's head football coach. Rudy had great success at FAMU. His biggest win occurred in Miami, where his team defeated the Division I Miami Hurricanes. That was the first time that a predominantly black football team played and defeated a Division I program.

Under Hubbard, FAMU was the first team to win the inaugural NCAA I-AA National Championship in 1978.

BACK TO JACKSONVILLE, AND THE WFL

The WFL's Jacksonville Sharks got off to a rocky start. Many of the team owners were not vetted very well and some did not have funds to pay their players or coaches. However, the WFL essentially "taxed" owners with adequate funding to help those franchises who could not pay their bills. The Sharks' owner, Fran Monaco, was one of those who was short of funds.

After eight games, the league took over the team, fired Monaco and Bud Asher, and hired Charlie Tate as the head coach. Eventually, the Sharks got new ownership, with Earl Knabb as principal owner. Dick Butkus, the former Chicago Bear star and NFL Hall of Famer, was also part of the ownership group. The team changed its name to the Jacksonville Express.

Mr. Knabb, who was a big man in the timber business, had more money than he could spend. However, he did not like the idea of paying for other teams in the league. After he took over, the Express lost more games than they won. I hoped we could last another season, but Mr. Knabb and several other substantial owners refused to subsidize those teams who could not pay their players. The league folded. I had a wife, a child, a new house, and no job.

I did some substitute teaching in Orange Park, a suburb of Jacksonville, before a great opportunity presented itself. While coaching with Jacksonville, each coach got the use of a car from a local dealer. My dealer was Conrad Hawkins, who owned a Chevrolet dealership.

He asked me whether I had ever considered selling cars. I took a sales job in his dealership and used the skills I had learned in recruiting which, in effect, is selling. I did so well that, after working for ten months, Conrad called me to his office. He told me he wanted to recommend me for the General Motors Dealership Development program, since GM was vigorously recruiting minority dealers. I was elated and I told him to make the recommendation.

Just before Christmas 1975, I learned I had been accepted in the program. I continued training at Conrad's dealership and was making excellent progress. In early March, Marv Braden called me. Marv and I worked together on Earle Bruce's staff at Iowa State. I kept in touch with Marv and most of the coaches with whom I worked because, in all honesty, I still had coaching in the back of my mind. After a few pleasantries, Marv said he was coaching at Michigan State and that Darryl Rogers needed a receivers coach. Marv wanted to know whether I was interested.

It took me about two seconds to say yes. Marv told me that spring practice started in a month and asked when I could come to Michigan. I could be there in a week.

The first call I made after that was to my wife, Pat, who was elated. Michigan was close to home and family.

Next, I went to Conrad's office. When I told him the news, he looked at me incredulously. He asked me, "Are you a damn fool, Ray? If you stay in this business, you will own a dealership in the next year or two and it won't be long before you can be a millionaire." I thanked him for all he had done for me and left his office and the dealership. To this day, he has not been able to wrap his head around my decision.

I have thought about that morning many times. I do not regret getting back into coaching. Though I didn't know that at the time I took the job, I would get to coach a player like Kirk Gibson.

MICHIGAN STATE SPARTANS AND THE WEST COAST OFFENSE

I arrived in Michigan the last week in March 1976. My wife stayed behind to sell our house. We had moved a lot and she really disliked having to handle all of the hard work and the children while I flew off to coach. However, I always appreciated all she did.

I was impressed with the coaching staff. Darryl Rogers was a West Coast guy—personable, easygoing, and an advocate of the Bill Walsh West Coast passing game. He left Michigan State a couple of years later to become the head coach of the NFL's Detroit Lions.

Sherman Lewis, a Michigan State All-American, was the secondary coach. Sherm had a long coaching career in the NFL with the San Francisco 49ers and Green Bay Packers. Another young coach on our staff was Ray Sherman. Ray was a graduate assistant at the time. However, he blossomed as a coach and landed positions with several professional teams. After several years with the 49ers and the Houston Oilers, he served as the offensive coordinator for the Green Bay Packers and Pittsburgh Steelers.

Michigan State was much different from Iowa State. The school had won a National Championship and had great tradition. However, the year before I got there, the university had received probation from the NCAA and was unable to compete in postseason play.

We had several outstanding athletes but not the depth to compete with Michigan, Notre Dame, Southern California, and Ohio State. We played well and had a winning season in 1976 and looked forward to the 1977 season. The first order of business was to recruit some quality athletes, and we did. In 1977, we were a much better football team. In 1978, we were Big Ten co-champions.

INVITATIONS FROM THE NORTHWEST

I interviewed for the head coaching position at the University of Oregon in 1977. Though I interviewed well and the panel said they were impressed, they hired Rich Brooks, who was an assistant at UCLA. The panel said Brooks was more familiar with the high school coaches in California. I couldn't argue with the choice. After eighteen years as the head coach for Oregon, he went on to jobs as the head coach of the St. Louis Rams, the defensive coordinator of the Atlanta Falcons, and the head coach at the University of Kentucky.

I also interviewed for the head coaching position at the University of Washington. However, in my mind, I wasn't given serious consideration because the interview was a result of the school being under some pressure to at least interview a black coach. I liked the thought of them making an effort, but token interviews were not what I had in mind with the effort I put in organizing the BCS. I never visited the Seattle campus. A representative flew to Michigan to interview me. The school ultimately hired Don James, a good friend of mine from my coaching days in Ohio.

TEMPTATION IN TEXAS

Each spring, the Dallas Cowboys sponsor a golf tournament for Division I head coaches. Darryl Rogers played in the tournament in the spring of 1977. When he returned to East Lansing, he called me into his office and told me that Fred Akers, the University of Texas head coach, wanted to talk with me about a job. I asked Darryl, jokingly, whether he was trying to get rid of me. He wasn't, but he thought it might be a great opportunity.

Texas had run the wishbone formation for several years and the fans were putting pressure on Akers to update his offense. After talking to Darryl, Akers learned about our offensive philosophy and was very interested in learning more, so Darryl recommended me to him.

He told Akers that I was his offensive coordinator and that I had a complete understanding of the passing game. He also mentioned that I was black. Texas did not have a black coach at the time.

Akers was fine with that because he was considering hiring a black assistant. Darryl told me that if I had any interest to call Coach Akers and arrange a flight to Austin, Texas to spend a few days with the Texas coaching staff.

I called Coach Akers the next day, and he had his secretary arrange my flight. I flew first class to Austin where I was met by a graduate assistant who took me to a very classy hotel. When I entered my room, the first thing I saw was a gigantic basket filled with fruit, cheese, salami rolls, candy, and two bottles of wine. "Welcome to Longhorn Country," read the note inside. The note had a picture of Bevo, the Longhorn mascot, embedded in it. They do things big in Texas.

I got comfortable in one of the two leather recliners, turned on the TV, and began sampling from the basket. I wanted to drink some of the wine but thought it would be better to drink after I settled in later that evening.

At about four in the afternoon, Coach Akers called to say he was waiting in the lobby. I told him I would be right down. I had seen him on TV but never in person. He was not an impressive-looking man but had the persona consistent with being the boss.

We shook hands and he outlined what was going to happen for the rest of the day. He was organized. About ten minutes after leaving the hotel, we were on the impressive Texas campus. As we drove through campus, I looked to my right and saw a working oil well. It was not the tall, pyramid type, so I thought it might be a prop or just a symbol of Texas oil. Coach Akers smiled and assured me it was real and owned by the university. The school had a money-making machine on campus.

We rode past the aquatic arena and toward the football facility. When we went into the meeting room, there were twelve people sitting around a large conference table. I was introduced to everyone but only remember the offensive coordinator's name—Leon Manley. Coach Akers said that he and Manley had been together for many years.

I was the only black person in the room.

The staff and I talked for a while. They asked the usual questions—my background in coaching, how did I think the Big Ten matched up to the Southwest Conference, etc. Then we got down to the real reason they had brought me there. Coach Akers asked me to go to the chalkboard and talk to them about our (MSU's) passing philosophy. I talked about a half-hour about my experience in the Run and Shoot offense before they started asking questions.

The protocol in this type of meeting dictates that the guy with chalk has to answer every question even if the same question is asked several times. In 1977, unlike now, few teams ran wide-open offenses with four and five receivers. Teaching these guys how it worked was like teaching players new to our philosophy.

Coach Manley asked the most questions. He was an old-school coach who could not wrap his head around how we could release both running backs into pass routes. He kept saying that they couldn't do that in the Southwest Conference, so I suggested bringing in films tomorrow to demonstrate what I talked about on the chalkboard against Big Ten and other opponents.

The meeting lasted about two hours before Coach Akers said it was time for us to go to dinner with the president of the Longhorn Club. The club, I learned, consisted of the big donors to the Texas program. On the way there, Coach Akers talked about the advantage of working at the University of Texas.

We were buzzed in through the gate and it took a while to drive down the road and up the winding driveway to the front of the impressive-looking mansion. The owner greeted us at the door. "Welcome, Coach Greene— glad to have you in the great state of Texas." He was a tall, handsome man who looked like my stereotype of a rich Texan. He did not have on a cowboy hat, but he was dressed in cowboy attire and was wearing Tony Llama boots. He reminded me of J. R. in the television series *Dallas*.

As we entered the enormous mansion, the only thing more impressive than the house itself was the beautiful and extravagant décor. The oil paintings, family portraits, Persian rugs, and tasteful, expensive furniture reminded me of a furniture store and did not look lived-in.

As we went into the den to have a drink before dinner, I saw a young black man walking in from the pool. As he got closer, I marveled at the young man's physique. I thought to myself: if I wanted to build a football player, he would look like this young man. As he entered the house, the Longhorn Club president called him over and Coach Akers said, "Coach Greene, I'd like for you to meet Earl Campbell." I reached to shake his hand and my hand was swallowed up in his grip. As I tried to squeeze his hand with as much pressure as I could, I recognized him as the All-American running back. At Michigan State, we did not have a running back who looked anything like Earl Campbell. I doubt whether anyone else did. Earl was cordial and continued on his way before we were shown into the dining room.

We were served a great dinner—steak, of course, baked potatoes, green beans, etc. After dinner we went to the den, where Cuban cigars were presented, lighted, and a cordial was served. They asked how I liked what I saw so far and what I thought of Earl. I told them he was an impressive young man.

They were convinced they were going to win the National Championship that fall, and I thought to myself that it was entirely possible. They went on to tell me I would receive a substantial raise and they would get my wife a job, even though they never inquired about what type work she did. They even promised to have an alumnus build us a house, and that I would have a lot of equity in it when I moved in. I enjoyed all the attention as they recruited me. We'd been at the mansion for about three hours when Coach Akers said it was time to go, saying we had a long day tomorrow.

When we got back to the hotel, we parked in front and Coach Akers said both he and the Longhorn Club president were impressed with the way I had handled myself. He told me what a great honor it would be to have me on his staff and that he liked what he saw during my meeting with his staff.

I have to admit, he had almost sold me. I went to my room, where I searched my basket for wine and cheese. I put my films in my duffel bag before retiring for the evening.

I woke up early, showered, dressed, and went to the coffee shop for a cup of coffee. As I was leaving, I walked out of the front entrance just as Coach Akers arrived. He was early and I was glad I was ready. He said he was going to take me to a place to have the best breakfast in Texas.

We drove for about fifteen minutes and entered what I guessed was Austin's seamy side. We finally pulled in front of a hole-in-the-wall restaurant. When we went inside, there was a small crowd and several people shouted, "Hey coach, how ya doin'?" It was obvious Coach Akers had been there before.

The server, a short, stubby black woman with a winning smile immediately came to the table. "What you gonna have, Coach? The special?"

He said, "You got it! And Ray," he commanded, "I want you to have the special too." It was his treat, so I said OK.

Most of the patrons were not black. There were several white men in business attire talking and enjoying breakfast. When our food arrived, there appeared to be enough for everyone in the restaurant—two platters loaded with French toast, eggs, bacon, sausage, grits, apple butter, and hot sauce.

Coach was right; it was a great breakfast. I tried valiantly but could not finish everything on my plate. I would definitely come back to this place if I decided to move to Austin. The meal only cost sixteen dollars. I wondered how the restaurant stayed in business serving that much food for so little. Coach Akers pulled out a wad of bills and left a fifty-dollar bill on the table. We then headed to the football offices.

When we arrived, the coaches began taking their seats around the huge conference table. I went to the board to review what I had talked about the previous day. Again, there were several questions. I told them to hold the questions and look at the film. That way, they would get a better understanding of what I had presented the day before.

Most major colleges make at least two or three copies of the offensive and defensive film on separate reels. They then make what are called *cut-ups* of each play. Let's say we call a Toss 48 play. Each Toss 48 play of every game is put on a separate reel. We then put all the Toss 48's against different defenses on the same reel. For example, if a team plays a four-man front, all of the Toss 48's against that defense are put on the same reel. We do this for every play we run.

I ran the first play on the reel. The play was 97 X, A-Under. It was a play where the quarterback reads the defense and anticipates a blitz from the man the tailback is supposed to block. This is called a *hot read*. At the line of scrimmage, he makes an alert call. When the tailback hears the call, instead of blocking his assigned defender, he runs a *hot route* in the void left by the blitzer.

I showed about ten plays that illustrate this technique. I then ran a reel of the same play, except the tailback's man does not blitz. Instead, the defender drops back to cover a pass route. In this scenario, since the tailback's man did not blitz, the tailback route adjustment is to run to an open spot between linebackers. Our reels included not only the successful plays, but also ones that were not successful. In those cases, I pointed out the mistakes made.

We had a good tailback, Rich Baes, who caught thirty-five of these types of passes and made a first down eighty-five percent of the time. Rich was only 5'9" and 185 pounds. I stopped the film and told the staff to imagine Earl Campbell catching the ball in the same position. "Hell, he would have probably scored on half of those plays," one coach responded.

We watched film for four hours before we took a break. Leon Manley, the offensive coordinator, sat silently through all of this. He was not convinced. During the break, I asked Coach Manley what he was thinking. He hesitated and said, "Coach, I still don't believe you can release those backs in this conference."

I told him, "Coach, you saw those plays against Michigan, Southern Cal, Ohio State, Penn State, and the rest of the Big Ten. If it worked against them, it will work here." He refused to budge. I decided then that I would not take the job. We watched some more film and everyone seemed impressed—except Manley.

When Coach Akers said it was time for me to go, he and I headed back to the hotel to get my luggage. On the way, he asked me whether I liked what I saw enough to come to Texas and be on his staff. I asked him about becoming the offensive coordinator, but he said that was Leon's job. "However," he said, "you can coordinate the passing game."

I could foresee a major problem. If there was conflict, I would come out on the short end. I told him that I was really impressed with everything but wanted to discuss it first with my family that now included my wife and two children.

"Why don't you call her now; we'll fly her down here tonight, and tomorrow you both can look at an area where you would like to have your home built." It was an enticing offer, but I had pretty much made up my mind. I told him I would get back to him tomorrow. He took me to the airport and an hour later I was on my way back to East Lansing.

When I got home, Pat told me that Coach Akers called and told her he really looked forward to meeting her when we come to Texas. He also told her about the salary and the house they were going to build for us. He really charmed her and she was impressed.

Pat was very excited until I told her that I was not going to accept the job. I told her that if I had taken that job, working with Coach Manley would eventually cause problems that might disrupt things. She was disappointed but said she understood. However, I don't think she did. I called Coach Akers the next day, as promised, and told him I was going to stay at Michigan State. He wished me well and said he enjoyed meeting me.

In the fall 1977, Texas won the National Championship and Earl Campbell won the Heisman Trophy.

EPILOGUE

Football, particularly college football, is the great unifier.

As I am writing this in 2015, the media is filled with comments about a situation that recently occurred at the University of Missouri. The chancellor and president resigned in response to student demands and a no confidence vote by the faculty.

The demands made by black and white students were a result of racist activities on the campus and the failure of the administration to act promptly to curtail them. They acted only after white and black members of the football team, and their coach, Gary Pinkel, joined the protests and threatened to boycott their upcoming game against Brigham Young University.

If the players had boycotted the game, it would have cost the university more than a million dollars. The students' demands included black faculty members, black student's safety on campus and more inclusion of black studies in the curriculum. This sounds strangely familiar to a time past.

I believe the resignations were prodded more by the loss of money than by the racist activities. I can't probe into the minds of the two administrators, but it is a sad commentary. This story is all too familiar to me because of what happened in athletic departments around the country in the mid- to late 1960s, when black coaches were the subject of black student-athletes' demands.

With blacks comprising more than fifty percent of the athletes on most major college basketball and football teams, I imagine there are many discussions going on now at the NCAA and among collegiate administrators about race, gender, and money.

Here is a scary thought. What if the teams in the NCAA Final Four basketball tournament decided to protest and threaten to boycott? The damage would be unimaginable. Think of the money the networks, hotels, restaurants, and sponsors would lose. This situation is not going unnoticed by the athletes at Northwestern University, who sued the NCAA to get monetary compensation, along with their scholarships, for playing football.

No matter their race, ethnicity, or economic status, millions of fans gather on autumn Saturdays for a specific purpose—to watch and cheer for their favorite teams.

*

As a skinny kid from a multicultural neighborhood in South Akron, Ohio, I had always wanted to play football, but I never thought I'd ever coach. In fact, I never knew I wanted to coach until the opportunity presented itself.

Having coached most of my career, I do not advise a young person to go into the profession unless there is an inner passion that tells him to coach. The long hours and pressure to be successful can be overwhelming. Families suffer the most because of the amount of time spent away from home. There were times, when my children were very young, that I left for work before they awakened and did not return until they were asleep. I had to learn to organize my free time to develop balance between my profession and my family. It can be done as long as your spouse is totally on board.

Not only has my experience been historically significant, it has taught me what is important in life. Winning is nice, and it certainly is better than losing, but it isn't everything. It is more important for players, particularly young players, to learn the principles that are necessary to succeed in life—hard work, sacrifice, selflessness, teamwork, and learning to rebound after disappointment.

A few coaches think the game is about them. I never did. I always believed the game was about teaching young men how to push themselves to the limit and understand the importance of being leaders and having a positive attitude. Of course, I like to win. However, I seldom mentioned winning to the young men I coached. Instead I stressed the importance of being successful on and off the field, being prepared, working hard, being truthful, and doing what they know is right.

Good character is the cornerstone of success but parents—not coaches or teachers—must take the lead in instilling good character in their children. I made it a practice to visit every recruit's home because I wanted to see how they treated their parents, siblings, and anyone else who lived in the house.

If I had any doubts about their character in those circumstances, I did not recruit them. I believe that if you recruit a hoodlum, four or five years later you will have an educated hoodlum. A coach can't undo bad habits or deviant behavior that parents have permitted over a period of eighteen or nineteen years. Of course, some youngsters do change. Once removed from their environment, some have an epiphany and see the need for change. However, I wouldn't bet on it. A look at the many recent negative incidents involving professional and collegiate athletes shows real-life examples that validate my opinion.

There was a time in my tenure when the powers-that-be didn't think black people would make great quarterbacks or coaches. Fortunately, that is one of the great changes I have witnessed. Football was not the only sport that went through that same kind of metamorphosis for black athletes. The story of Jackie Robinson's entry into Major League Baseball in 1947 is well chronicled. In basketball, there were blacks who played professionally before the NBA was formed in 1949. However, it was not until 1950 when Chuck Cooper, who was black, was drafted by the Boston Celtics, that basketball began to change.

The Washington Capitols (the old NBA team) also selected Earl Lloyd and Harold Hunter in 1950. While Lloyd was one of the first to break the color barrier in the NBA, his accomplishment was not nearly as well acclaimed as when Robinson broke Major League Baseball's color barrier. Lloyd said he endured his fair share of racism, including fans asking to see his tail, people telling him to go back to Africa, and some even spitting on him.

There was concern among some NBA owners that fans would not purchase expensive season tickets to watch teams comprised primarily of black athletes. This led some to believe there was a gentleman's agreement to put a quota system on the number of blacks on each team. The Boston Celtics and Red Auerbach followed this agreement until they drafted Bill Russell in the early 1960s. The Celtics would later become the first NBA team to start five black players and hire the league's first black head coach—Bill Russell.

The reality of blacks dominating the NBA is a concern to some for attendance reasons. Former NBA great Larry Bird, when he was the Indiana Pacers' president of basketball operations, stated in 2004 that the league needed more white players, because the league's fans are mostly white. "If you just had a couple of white guys in there, you might get [the fans] a little excited," said Bird, who is white. "But it is a black man's game, and it will be forever. I mean, the greatest athletes in the world are African American."

Meanwhile, those managing collegiate football today are more concerned than ever about the health of players. They have taken steps to limit contact in practice and to govern tackling technique to avoid concussions and other injuries. They are working on these things at all levels from youth football to the pros. That can only make for healthier players during and after their playing days. Professional football has finally come to the realization that they, too, have to change some of the rules to protect the safety of its players. It took the deaths of some famous players and scientific research for them to make player safety a priority.

Players' behavior on and off the field is also more closely monitored. There are stricter and more widely enforced academic standards for collegiate athletes. More severe penalties are now administered against players who behave badly on or off the field. Several professional players have lost careers because of spousal abuse and other negative acts. Not all athletes will become perfect people as a result, but more of them might be inclined to behave better if they knew their careers would be impacted by their actions.

My urban upbringing could have led me down some wrong paths. Thanks largely to my mother, I didn't stray too far off course. I was not a big problem for her because I liked school. In addition to the great teachers and coaches, I also had a great peer mentor in one of my childhood friends—Selma Gamble. Selma, who lived half a block from me on Miami Street, was a couple of years ahead of me in high school.

When he finished high school, he received a football scholarship to Miami University in Ohio. While he was away at school, he would often call to keep me up-to-date on how he was doing and encourage me to me keep "on track" academically. His advice and concern was instrumental in helping me earn a scholarship and be the first in my family to attend college.

As a child, I didn't appreciate the richness of my diverse neighborhood as much as I do now. Though some folks fell into typical traps with alcohol, drugs, and so forth, most people, though not highly educated, owned their own homes, worked hard for a living, and raised good kids. Today, if a young person is fortunate enough to have the same experience as I did growing up, he should be very thankful.

As for the changes in the game, when I played and coached, not much thought was given to the problems of concussions, domestic violence, and other hot topics in football or society at large. These situations no doubt existed but were not publicized. Thanks to modern communication, the women's movement, and public awareness of the danger, progress in addressing them is taking place.

In football, the phrase "got his bell rung" was used often and players were given smelling salts and continued playing. Looking back, I am amazed more athletes who played then did not die prematurely or have serious problems in later life. People expected a football player to get hit and hit hard on the field, but did not condone hurting women or others weaker than him.

I began my college coaching career in the late 1960s, in the era of "free love," LSD, and marijuana. I am certain some athletes were involved in that behavior. Fortunately, staff I worked with never had to deal with any of those problems. We have also seen more use of drugs—not only the performance enhancers, but also illegal recreational drugs among players. I played with several teammates who smoked cigarettes or drank beer, but I can't recall anyone I played with using illegal drugs.

When I became a head coach, there had been several nationally publicized cases about professional and collegiate athletes using steroids to enhance their strength. Some coaches did little to prevent it because their athletes were getting bigger and stronger.

One of the most prominent examples is Lyle Alzado, the great defensive end who played fifteen NFL seasons with the Denver Broncos, Cleveland Browns, and the then Los Angeles Raiders. His story was chronicled on the ESPN program "30 for 30." The effects of his steroid use did not show up until he was done with football.

My athletes knew how I felt about drugs. I had some suspects, but we never had any problems of which I was aware. We had random drug testing, implemented after discussion, with the consent of the athletes.

Training and medical decisions are different. As a player, I was given excellent medical attention when needed. But, the sport emphasized being "tough." Many players did not report what they considered "small" hurts and pains, which led to serious injuries. Athletic trainers and team doctors now require treatment on even the smallest of injuries.

Many parents today and some medical professionals are suggesting that children should not play football because recent scientific studies show that too much contact increases the danger of concussions.

That is true. In soccer, a rule recently changed to prohibit children younger than eleven years of age from heading the ball. I believe this rule will cause the quality of US soccer to decline because players will not master a required technique at a young age. Still, I agree with the rule even though studies have shown that the great majority of concussions in soccer occur after player-to-player collisions, rather than after heading the ball.

In the last few years, many concussion studies have led to several football rule changes. Generally, concussion problems result from multiple hits to the head, rather than a single hit during a game. Therefore, practice times have been shortened and coaches have been instructed to conduct fewer full-contact drills in practice. Players are now taught to not lead with head when tackling an opponent. A new penalty called *targeting* requires ejection from the game if a player leads with the head during a tackle. Doctors on the sideline now determine whether a player should continue playing after a head injury using what is termed "concussion protocol." These are steps in the right direction.

I would advise parents to allow their children to play football if their children want to play. However, parents should know the coach and his past practices in working with children. Regardless of how meticulous a coach is and how much he cares about children's safety, a child can get seriously injured. However, a child can get injured riding a bicycle, skateboarding, or in many other activities. Many parents are not letting their children participate in football. Will this eventually hurt the game? I don't know. However, in working with youth football for the past twenty years in the city of Huntsville, I have not seen one serious injury or know of any child who now suffers from a head injury suffered in football. On a personal level, the only serious injury I have had is a broken arm when I stumbled and fell off our front porch.

In college, athletes don't get paid. At least, they don't get paid legally. They get scholarships that cover room, board, books, fees, and tuition. Most would think that is sufficient for a collegiate athlete. Until recently, scholarship athletes were not allowed to work during the season. Because of that, some have casually taken money from boosters.

That may begin to change. Recently, as previously mentioned, athletes from Northwestern University sued the NCAA, asking for what I consider a reasonable stipend for playing sports. One side of the argument says the athletes are amateurs and not employees of the university. Athletes argue that they bring big money into the university with their performances on the field and they should share in that bounty.

I tend to side with the athletes. Universities use athletes' names and images to sell tickets, jerseys, T-shirts, concessions, and other paraphernalia, bringing in millions of dollars. If an athlete sells such items on his own or signs his name for a fee, he is declared ineligible. I believe that if an athlete's talent or image is used to make someone else money, he should get a cut of the proceeds.

Free tuition, books, etc., don't fully compensate the athlete. Athletic shoe companies pay head coaches large sums of money to have their teams wear the company's shoes. Coaches get paid, but the athletes who advertise the product every time they play get nothing.

The athletes most affected by the current rules are those from low and/or middle-income families. I can only estimate, and I think accurately, from my coaching experience, that more than half of the athletes, black and white, come from such families. Parents of most athletes can't afford to send money on a regular basis for items such as laundry, movies, clothing, or an occasional date. Scholarships provide none of these things.

Having children who went through college, I can attest that students need money for things outside of what the NCAA allows. I can foresee rules changing to help these athletes, especially at the major institutions.

Most athletes never become professional athletes. According to 2019 NCAA statistics, approximately 73,557 athletes are now playing collegiate football. Of those, 16,346 are eligible to be drafted by the NFL. There are only 256 draft slots. Of those who are drafted, only a small percentage will actually earn a living playing football. Only a few get a shot to make an NFL team as a non-drafted free agent. Fewer still actually make the team and play for a decent number of years.

Coaches, parents, and others who influence these athletes should emphasize that they are in college not just to play sports, but also to get an education, graduate, and become well-rounded, productive adults. I believe those who make decisions in collegiate athletics will find the right balance to properly reward athletes for their performance while still providing what they need to become good citizens.

At the pro level, the contracts have gotten astronomical for the great players. To me, this is fair because I believe a person should be paid proportionally for the service he delivers. It is the athletes, coaches, and staff who provide the product that enriches owners. NBA great Shaquille O'Neal summed it up during an interview when the reporter asked him if he was a rich man. Shaq responded: "I am not rich! The man who pays my salary is rich."

Today, players have gotten bigger, faster, and stronger than ever before. Thirty years ago, there were few linemen—on offense or defense—who topped 250 pounds. Now, they routinely top 300 pounds. Running backs are as big as linemen used to be, and some tight ends are the same size as linemen.

The difference is that these big guys can run fast and are agile. When big and fast people run into each other, there will be injuries. Now, because of improved training methods, weight training, improved equipment, diet and rule changes, there are fewer injuries than in the past.

Today, offense, particularly passing offense, is king. But, as much as I love the passing game, I believe that to win consistently, a team must have a great kicking game, an effective running game, and a great defense.

In the National Championship game between Auburn and Oregon several years ago, Oregon had the most prolific offense in the nation, averaging forty-nine points a game. Auburn won the title because its defense made Oregon look inept.

I also believe that an effective passing game increases the capability to run the ball. When I coached high school football, we ran the Run and Shoot offense. It was an offense in which smaller linemen could scramble-block and be successful. It was fun to practice and fun for fans to watch. We had athletes who may not have been able to play at other schools in our city, yet they were good enough to get us to the championship game.

With two or three good athletes at receiver, running back and quarterback, and with a team that can effectively use the techniques coaches teach them with few mistakes, a team can win a championship. We never knew how an opponent was going to defend us, but during the first quarter, we could figure it out and adjust accordingly.

My experience playing and coaching football was more than fulfilling on several levels. My journey into major collegiate football was surprising to many who knew the kid from Miami Street in South Akron. It never seemed like a big deal to me. However, I must admit that if someone had told me when I was a youngster that I would achieve what I did, I would not have believed it.

Football gave me the opportunity to travel to places I had only dreamed about. It also paid for my education, gave me the opportunity to be associated with many great people, and provided me the means to give my family a great life.

If more youngsters today would understand that football and sports are not the be-all and end-all, but rather a catalyst to a great and productive life, perhaps they would give more attention to being better students. Coaches, with the control they have, can and must play a major role in that endeavor.

Despite not achieving my goal to be a head coach in the National Football League, I had a good run.

Though the game has changed with time, the unifying aspect of it, fortunately, has not. After the games on autumn Saturdays, people go back to their normal lives, their prejudices, and so forth. But for those few hours on a Saturday afternoon, they are of one mind—rooting their team on to victory.

I witnessed an example of that one Saturday morning in Lincoln, Nebraska. I was there to scout Nebraska who was playing Oklahoma State. I awakened about nine to go to the hotel restaurant for breakfast.

I was walking through the lobby wearing my Iowa State blazer when an older, silver-haired lady, wearing a red blazer and a big red cowboy hat with a white "N" on it, stopped me. She cordially inquired why I was in Lincoln. I told her I was from Iowa State scouting Nebraska because we were going to play them next week.

She looked at me and said, "Good luck son! This afternoon we are going to beat these chumps and next week, we are going to come over to Ames and kick your ass!" No doubt she was a grandmother and a Christian woman. On Saturdays, she was a "Cornhusker Football Fanatic." On top of that, what she said came true.

Football is a great game, in which young men compete in hundreds of mini-battles, man-to-man, for sixty minutes, regardless of the weather. They play hard for their fans and for each other. There are rivalries and some teams dislike each other, but there is no hate as some would infer. After the game, they look their adversaries in the eye, shake hands, and wish them well. Whether they have experienced the joy of victory or the agony of defeat, their thoughts almost immediately turn to next week's opponents.

That's football, and I am happy to have contributed in some small way to the game.

Appendix

UNIVERSITY OF AKRON INTRAMURALS

The intramural program at The University of Akron was a popular student activity. I participated in the basketball and wrestling programs. I played basketball in high school, but South High School did not have a wrestling program, so I had to learn everything in a physical education class I took during my freshman year at the university. Coach Andy Maluke, our defensive line coach in football, was the head wrestling coach and the instructor for the class. After the class, Coach Maluke tried to convince me to try out for the team, but I declined. I did not mind hard work, but that sport is unlike any other and I did not want to put in the time. In intramurals, I made it to the finals where I had to wrestle Tom Lowery. Tom played linebacker on the football team. He also, I learned later, was one of the best wrestlers in the state as a high school wrestler. As a matter of fact, I found out during our match. I had only learned a few moves and he countered each one. During the first period I did okay by using my speed and quickness. I got a takedown and scored three points when I gained control; however, in the second period, I ran out of moves. From the down position, I tried a rollout. Out-gunned in the technical aspect of that move, I ended up on my back and got pinned. That ended my wrestling career.

Intramural basketball was a different story. Our basketball team, The DRGs—an acronym for Dave and Ray Greene—won the championship every year. (Dave is not a relative, but everyone thought we were and we let them.) When freshmen football players reported to camp, Dave and I would start recruiting for our basketball team. We would find out who could play and have them commit to playing with us. That meant that each year we had the best white and black athletes on campus as members of the DRGs. The fraternities were so frustrated that they organized their own tournament to decide a fraternity championship because they could not beat the DRGs. Each year we would lose most of our team to fraternities, so we would just start over. It was a great system.

In my junior year, I got a job as the assistant director of intramurals. I was responsible for hiring officials. I also officiated basketball games. In most cases, there would be a problem being on a team and also serving as an official; however, none of the teams complained. They accused me at times of making a bad call, but none ever accused me of showing any bias. I had the reputation of being a fair official.

One of the biggest games on campus was the fraternity championship game. Invariably, the two best teams were the Lone Star and Phi Delta Theta Fraternities. Joe Mackey, our quarterback, DRG alumni, and a Lone Star member, and Jim Semester, a Phi Delta Theta member and former classmate at South High, came to the intramural office to speak with me. Both played on the football team. They asked me if I would be willing to referee the fraternity championship game. This was a heated rivalry and they thought I would be the best referee for the game.

I don't remember who won the game. During the game, the coaches yelled at me a few times, but nothing out of the ordinary. After the game several members from both teams congratulated me on a good game and invited me to the after parties.

During my coaching career, I have often thought about my experience as a referee in intramurals when I have had to make a controversial decision. I just say to myself, "Greene, call 'em like you see 'em both ways and everything will work out."

GREENE'S FORMER PLAYERS AND COACHING ASSOCIATES

Below are a few of the young men, among the hundreds I have coached who distinguished themselves in football and/or business:

Players	Football After College	Job After College
Larry Addison	Prison Warden	
Don Plusquellic		Mayor of Akron
Howard Ballard	Buffalo Bills, Seattle Seahawks	Teacher and High School Coach, Private Business
Kirk Gibson	Detroit Tigers, Los Angeles Dodgers Manager of Arizona Diamondbacks	
Reginald Gipson	Seattle Seahawks	Private Business
Isaiah "Ike" Harris	St. Louis Cardinals	Vice-President Bell Telephone, Retired
Ted Hendricks	Baltimore Colts, Oakland Raiders (Hall of Fame)	
Barry Hill	Miami Dolphins	
Otto Stowe	Miami Dolphins, Dallas Cowboys, Denver Broncos	
Ananias Harris	Pittsburgh Steelers	
Ted Jornov	Jacksonville Sharks	
Lewis Tillman	New York Giants, Chicago Bears	
Brick Haley	Coach, Troy State, Georgia Tech, Chicago Bears, LSU, Texas, Arkansas	
Houston Hoover	Atlanta Falcons	
Jeff Toney	Seattle Seahawks	
Ernest French	Pittsburg Steelers	Minister
Thomas Hopkins	Cleveland Browns	Private Business
Keith Krepfle	Philadelphia Eagles	Private Business
Zefross Moss	New England Patriots	Private Business
Dwight Wright	Buffalo Bills	Real Estate Development
Barry Wagner	Arena Football	
Mike Williams	Washington Redskins	
Raymond Cole	Los Angeles Rams	

Many more were on NFL teams but did not make a final roster. This is a very small percentage of the young men with whom I have worked. Most have gone on to become good family men and positive contributors to their communities.

Coaches with whom I worked or were on my coaching staffs. Several have had outstanding careers.

Coaches	
Joe Avezzano	Assistant Coach-Iowa State, Pittsburgh University, Dallas Cowboys, Head Coach-Oregon State
Johnny Majors	Assistant Coach-Mississippi State, Head Coach-Iowa State, Pittsburgh, Tennessee
Earle Bruce	Head Coach-Tampa, Iowa State, Ohio State
John Chavis	Defense Coordinator-Alabama A&M, Alabama State, Tennessee, LSU, Texas A&M, Arkansas Razorbacks
Darryl Rogers	Head Coach-San Jose State, Arizona State, Michigan State, Detroit Lions
Brick Haley	Assistant Coach-Alabama A&M, Troy State, Georgia Tech, Chicago Bears, LSU, Univ. of Texas, Missouri
Jimmy Johnson	Assistant Coach-Iowa State, Head Coach: Okla. State, Miami (National Champs), Dallas Cowboys (Super Bowl Winner), Miami Dolphins
Sherman Lewis	Assistant Coach-Michigan State, SF 49'ers, Green Bay Packers, Pittsburgh Steelers, St. Louis Rams
Ray Sherman	Assistant Coach-Georgia, Michigan State, Houston Oilers, Green Bay, Pittsburgh Steelers (Offensive Coordinator), St. Louis Rams
Woodrow McCorvey	Offensive Coordinator-Alabama A&M, North Carolina Central,) Alabama-Assistant Head Coach, Tennessee, Miss. State, South Carolina, Clemson (Asst. Athletic Dir.)
C. T. Hewgley	Assistant Coach—Michigan State, Miami, Michigan State, Kansas City Chiefs
Curtis Harris	Assistant Coach-Alabama A&M
Tyrone Willingham	Assistant Coach-Michigan State, North Carolina State, Head Coach-Stanford, Notre Dame, Washington State
Andrew Lee	Assistant Coach, Central State, Alabama A&M
John Montgomery	Alabama A&M, Wichita State, Cincinnati
George Haffner	Offensive Coordinator—Iowa State, Assistant Coach—Georgia
W. C. Gorden	Head Coach-Jackson State

Darrell Rogers	Head Coach–San Jose State, Michigan State, Arizona State, Detroit Lions
Jackie Sherrill	Defensive Coordinator–Iowa State, Assistant Coach–Alabama, Head Coach–Washington State, Pittsburgh, Mississippi State, and Texas A&M
Charlie Tate	Assistant Coach–Georgia Tech, Head Coach–University of Miami, Jacksonville Sharks
Mike Riley	Head Coach–Winnipeg, Blue Bombers, Oregon State, University of Nebraska

ACCOLADES

Entering a door previously closed by the restraints of race almost always requires the assistance of many others. Therefore, as one of the first black coaches in Division I college football, I must pay homage to those individuals who were instrumental in my journey. Because of them, I had the opportunity to work with some great coaches and coach some outstanding athletes. Several of those athletes have gone on to become successful professionals in business and professional sports. Many of the coaches with whom I worked have excelled as collegiate and professional football coaches. Following are their perspectives on my career.

From Johnny Majors

Working for Hall of Fame Coach Frank Broyles at the University of Arkansas in 1967 had opened up opportunities for assistant coaches on his staff to become head coaches. Then, Iowa State University's Athletic Director, Clay Stapleton, a University of Tennessee graduate, as I was, invited me to interview for his head coaching job in football. Iowa State had had several losing seasons. I wasn't immediately interested in visiting because Iowa State had been referred to as "a football graveyard," and I had no interest in moving north.

The Cyclones had never won a championship or played in a bowl game in its history, but with Stapleton's urging, I interviewed. At my first press conference after accepting the job, and having expressed my appreciation to Iowa State and its administration, the press conference was opened for questions.

The first question to me was, "Coach Majors, how are you going to handle the black players?"

It was quite evident someone had researched my coaching and playing background. My whole career was spent in the South, with the exception of a rookie football season in 1957 in the Canadian Football League with the Montreal Alouettes. That team had approximately a half-dozen black players. I was born and raised in two tiny towns in lower Middle Tennessee: Lynchburg (population 350) and Huntland (population 300). Both were segregated and predominantly white.

Most reasonable or knowledgeable people realize that black people had little or no opportunity compared to whites. I played with black kids growing up in Lynchburg many times and we had fun together. Looking back, it is too bad that we couldn't have gone to school together, even with the strong possibility I would have been a second or third teamer behind the twins, L. B. and J. B. McGowan. Now, the twins are 81 years old, which I will be May 21, 2016. I rarely have ever returned to Lynchburg without seeing my twin black friends who have been loyal for 81 years. We loved each other.

Having played at Tennessee from 1953 to 1956, coached there from 1957 through 1959 and at Mississippi State from 1960 to 1967 (all segregated at the time), my reply to the Iowa media was, "I don't really know how I will handle the black athletes and only time will tell; however, I will treat them the same as any other player on the team. When they make a good play, I will pat them on the butt and say, 'good job' or 'great job,' and if they mess up, I will correct them on the spot as firmly as I see fit at the time."

Regardless of the kind of man I am today or have been through life, I know this: I never heard my parents or relatives ever use a bad word or term in addressing a black person. We all showed respect for our black friends and that respect was mutual.

I accepted the Iowa State head coaching job in December 1967. I was the youngest head coach in Division I-A at age 32. I assembled an exciting and very young coaching staff, and several would become successful collegiate head coaches. Larry Lacewell (Arkansas State), Ollie Keller (University of Louisiana—Monroe), Jimmy Johnson (Oklahoma State, University of Miami (Fla.), Dallas Cowboys and Miami Dolphins), Jackie Sherrill (Washington State, University of Pittsburgh, Texas A&M and Mississippi State and Joe Avezzano (Oregon State) were all on the staff. A total of thirty-two future college or NFL head coaches worked on my staff as they advanced in the profession.

In 1968, my first year, we made slight progress. We only won three games which was one win better than the 1967 team. Although our team was undersized, they gave great effort and we were competitive in every game. The enthusiasm and effort displayed by our team and coaches established a new and exciting attitude that energized our supporters throughout the state of Iowa.

My philosophy was, "We will play with pride and enthusiasm, and we will never give up or learn to lose. We will dress like winners, we will act like winners, we will practice like winners and will play like winners, and then we will learn to win."

Our coaches, players, and fans bought into this and maintained it for five years. We laid the foundation that developed into bowl invitations in 1971 and 1972, the first in school history.

Things became more exciting in 1969 when I hired two new young coaches, Ray Greene and Joe Avezzano.

I have had many people ask me through the years if coaching got tougher during the last few years of my career and now. I don't think that it has.

I believe the time when I became head coach at Iowa State was the toughest times of all because in 1967 we were encountering the first of the drug culture in America and certainly on college campuses. The Vietnam War was in some of its hottest times and was putting tremendous pressure on male college students with the draft. Also, there were numerous black boycotts on university campuses. Prior to that time coaches only had to deal with alcohol, tobacco, and a few bar fights.

Now here were bombings of the University of Wisconsin and University of Iowa ROTC armories to protest the Vietnam War and sit-ins and protests at campus executive offices at Columbia University, Iowa State University, and others.

At other universities—Syracuse, Michigan State, Iowa, Iowa State, Wisconsin, Wyoming, University of Washington—to name a few, students demanded the hiring of black coaches, administrators, and other upper-echelon positions on campuses.

Iowa State had around twenty thousand students; approximately two hundred were black, many of whom were student-athletes. The black students were certainly reasonable and as a result, Dr. William Bell from

North Carolina A&T, a predominately black school, was hired as a vice president for student affairs.

That was a great appointment and Dr. Bell was one of the most wonderful men I have ever worked with. He was the first black administrator in Iowa State University's history. I certainly realized the necessity to hire an African American coach and told the boycotting students that I would hire a black coach following the 1968 football season.

I had already filled my staff positions for the 1968 spring practice and the fall seasons. I was limited to six varsity coaches, a freshman coach, and a scout team coach. I also told the students, our team, and the administrators that I knew of no black assistant coaches at that time.

Fortunately, the football players did not boycott spring practice in 1968 even though many of them showed up for the meetings of the students, administrators, and coaches. Some of what I inherited at Iowa State needed vast improvement, including the relationship between the team and the African American students on campus.

I also needed a new athletic trainer, who is one of the most important people on the team because of his daily contact with the players.

I learned that, on occasion, when a black player came in to check on a bruise or injury with the head trainer, he would say things to them such as, "You don't look injured to me; you're already black and blue." I put a stop to that immediately.

Also, my secretary told me after practice one day that she and the (former) trainer had made a bet with each other. She said, "Coach Majors, the trainer and I made a bet and he is going to pay me $5 for every game we win and I'm going to pay him $5 for every game we lose."

She was very excited and certainly I knew right away that she was "on our team." The trainer was gone for good following spring practice and that was one the best moves of my career! There are certain parts of the "house" (organization) you have to clean up when you're the head coach. Some of the people you inherit in a new job will say, "We've never done it like this before and can't change."

There are others who respond and may suggest different ways to do things. But they also say, "Coach, whatever it takes and whatever you decide to do, we'll get it done!" I kept only one coach from the previous staff, and I hired all the rest.

To the best of my memory, only two black players decided to leave our program following 1968 spring practice, Willie Muldrew from Chicago, who was the best defensive lineman and one of the best players on the team. Unfortunately, Muldrew was shot and killed by his former girlfriend in the summer.

I released the trainer and had committed myself to hiring an African American assistant coach following the 1968 season.

I did not know many black coaches. I had met Coach Jake Gaither, the famous and heralded head football coach at Florida A&M, the predominately black university in Tallahassee, and Coach John Merritt, a highly successful coach at Tennessee State University in Nashville, another predominately black school.

I also got to know Buddy Young, one of football's all-time great black football players who had played at the University of Illinois and in the NFL. Buddy, at the time, was a key officer in the NFL. All of these renowned coaches provided me some early leads toward finding the best African American assistant coach.

Soon after I began my private search for the coach, I received a call from one of my favorite people: Coach LeRoy Pearce. He had been the outstanding receiver coach at the University of Tennessee while I was a player there in 1955 and 1956.

LeRoy gave me one of the biggest breaks in my life. He told me about Ray Greene, a young African American assistant coach who had worked at Dan McCarty High school in Fort Pierce, Florida. Dan McCarty had just been integrated in 1967 and Ray was their first black teacher and coach. LeRoy told me that he was now a student assistant at the University of Miami for Coach Charlie Tate. LeRoy Pearce was an assistant coach at Miami at the time.

Ray had received a scholarship at Miami to complete a graduate studies program designed to train administrators to work in multicultural schools. He had volunteered to work with the football team.

Because of my great confidence and respect for Coach Pearce, I contacted Coach Greene shortly after the 1968 season to interview him for the vacant scout team coaching position.

Coach Pearce had emphasized Coach Greene's ability and potential; his talents in teaching and leadership; and his confidence, energy, integrity, and enthusiasm. Coach Pearce's very important final statement said, "I'll guarantee you he can recruit and bring athletic talent to your program."

I was already impressed with what I had heard from Coach Pearce, but that final sentence rang the bell for me because we needed talented football players at Iowa State. The state of Iowa produced a limited number of high school prospects (normally a dozen top-notch recruits yearly), and we needed sixteen to eighteen to have a top-notch recruiting class.

I decided very early to recruit in Chicago, Wisconsin, Minnesota, New Jersey, and New York. I also thought it important to recruit in the South, especially in Georgia and Florida, because of the many talented black athletes available there. In 1969, southern universities were recruiting a bare minimum of black players. Kentucky recruited its first black player in 1966 and Tennessee its first in 1967. The other Deep South schools waited a while longer.

For example, Alabama recruited its first black player, John Mitchell, in 1971. I believe Florida, Mississippi, and Louisiana schools recruited their first black players even later.

In hiring Ray Greene and Joe Avezzano the same year, I ended up with two of the best recruiters in the nation. Plus, they both turned out to be outstanding coaches. I've never had two better hires in one year. Both of them moved to varsity positions the following year—Greene as receiver coach and Avezzano as offensive line coach.

In 1971 and 1972, Iowa State played in two postseason bowl games, the Sun Bowl and the Liberty Bowl. In my twenty-nine years as a head coach, I've never had two better recruiters and coaches on my staff than Ray and Joe. They and their wives, both beautiful women and lovely ladies, also brought some fresh and colorful new life to Ames, Iowa.

The state of Iowa was 98% white at the time. The entire town and campus loved the Greenes and their two children, Stephanie and Ray II.

Ray was the first black coach in the Big Eight Conference, and I'm quite certain he was the first black member of both the Ames Country Club and the Ames Elks Club. I could never repay LeRoy Pearce totally for putting me in touch with Ray Greene.

Players that Ray Greene recruited to Iowa State included Arlen Ciechanowski (linebacker and center–Georgia); Ted Jornov (linebacker, co-captain–New York); Willie Jones (wide receiver–Georgia); "Big Daddy"

Lawrence Hunt (defensive tackle–Florida); Henry Lewis (offensive tackle–Florida); Mike Strachan and Moses Moore (running backs–Florida); and Barry Hill (defensive back–Florida). As receivers coach, Ray also coached one of the best recruiting classes in Iowa State history, including Ike Harris (Tennessee); Willie Jones (Georgia) and Keith Krepfle (Wisconsin).

I followed Ray Greene's outstanding coaching career with the Jacksonville Sharks professional football team, Michigan State University, and the great job he did in building two outstanding football programs as head coach at North Carolina Central and at Alabama A&M. Ray Greene is a coach for all seasons and all teams.

Johnny Majors spent 29 years as a collegiate head coach, including stops at Iowa State University, the University of Pittsburgh, and the University of Tennessee.

From Former Athlete, Dwight Wright

In the past fifty years, a number of notable pioneers in the sport of football have helped make the game the most popular sport in America today. For every one that we've heard about, many trailblazers have flown unheralded under the radar, while making significant contributions behind the scenes.

This book is about Coach Ray Greene's groundbreaking journey—one that began growing up in Akron, Ohio, to becoming one of the first African American assistant coaches in Division 1 and pro football, and to finishing his career as head coach at a historically black university.

Coach Greene made a difference at every stop of his distinguished career by developing young men and coaches, standing up for fairness, standing on principles, and challenging those around him to do the right thing on and off the field, while winning football games the right way.

When I think about Coach Greene, a lot of words and phrases come to mind: intelligence, class, leader, teacher, integrity, character, morals, fairness, trust, developer of young men and coaches, demander of excellence, and a great football mind, just to name a few.

As an eighteen-year-old, I strolled onto the campus of Alabama A&M University on a football scholarship, not knowing what to expect from college football and a new head coach in his first season at the helm of the Bulldog football program.

Five years later, I left there with an enhanced self-awareness of what it meant to be a leader and a student-athlete, and I was better prepared for life and a career after college. Ray Greene inspired me and my teammates to excellence on and off the field, and he showed us how to achieve success the right way.

During a time when much discussion centered on athletes not getting their degrees, over eighty-two percent of his players graduated. His teachings helped me become a successful manager at a Fortune 50 company, and then founding and leading my own successful company.

Coach Greene also helped develop his assistant coaches. A number of the assistants on his Bulldog staff from my years under his guidance went on to make a name for themselves as coordinators in Division 1 football: most notably, Woody McCorvey and John Chavis.

Coach Greene was not a win-at-any-cost type of coach. He believed in winning the right way, even if it put him at a disadvantage. I remember an incident in college when he suspended our best player for a game against our biggest rival for missing curfew. This was the kind of game that gets coaches fired for losing.

Coach saw our teammate from a distance after curfew. He could have easily pretended not to see him, but he was fair and honest with himself and the rest of the team and suspended the player.

Recently, I was told a story by Gene Huey, a longtime NFL and college coach, about a time when he and Coach Greene were both young assistants in the Big Eight Conference (Nebraska and Iowa State). Both were at the AFCA Convention when a rumor surfaced that a black coach at one of the other conference universities had been violating recruiting rules.

Gene said that Coach Greene addressed the issue head on with the alleged violator and made it clear how his actions would impact the young players' perception of other African American coaches that were doing it the right way and of others to follow. That is the Coach Ray Greene that I know and respect.

Dwight Wright played for the Buffalo Bills in the NFL. He's now a businessman in Indianapolis, Indiana.

From Jimmy Johnson, Former Collegiate and Professional Football Coach

I first met Ray Greene when he joined our coaching staff at Iowa State University. Although I had never worked on a staff that included an African American, I have always believed that a man's character and ability are more important than his ethnicity or the color of his skin.

Early on, I learned Ray was an intelligent man who possessed excellent character and integrity. He was also a good football coach and recruiter, a hard worker, and a good family man. Many of the young men he recruited played major roles in our success.

At the time Ray joined the ISU staff, black athletes at many universities around the country were protesting their treatment and demanding the hiring of black coaches and other athletic staff. Ray made it clear that he was not at Iowa State to handle those type of problems. Fortunately, we never had those problems. I believe Ray's presence on our staff and his approach to working with all of our players helped us become closer as a team.

Equally important, Ray was a gentleman and he and his wife, Pat, were great assets in our staff's social interaction with alumni and supporters of the program.

Jimmy Johnson won two Super Bowls as head coach of the Dallas Cowboys and was also head coach of the Miami Dolphins in the National Football League. He won a national championship as head coach of the University of Miami Hurricanes. Today he is a football analyst with Fox Sports.

Ray Greene was born and raised in Akron, Ohio. He graduated from the University of Akron, where he double-majored in English and Telecommunication and Health, Recreation, and Physical Education. He holds a Master's Degree in Education Administration and Supervision from the University of Miami and currently resides in Huntsville, Alabama. Greene, as well as being a Hall of Fame football player at Akron, participated in track, campus politics, theatre, and debate. He hosted "Musical Theater" on the campus radio station, and he has played jazz piano his entire life. Coaching was not in his plans after graduation. But circumstance, or perhaps divine intervention, propelled him into a profession previously unavailable to those of his race.

Printed in the United States
By Bookmasters